THE CAUSES OF THE
AMERICAN REVOLUTION

Problems in American Civilization

READINGS SELECTED BY THE
DEPARTMENT OF AMERICAN STUDIES
AMHERST COLLEGE

Puritanism in Early America

The Causes of the American Revolution

The Declaration of Independence and the Constitution

Hamilton and the National Debt

The Turner Thesis concerning the Role of the Frontier in American History

Jackson versus Biddle — The Struggle over the Second Bank of the United States

The Transcendentalist Revolt against Materialism

Slavery as a Cause of the Civil War

Democracy and the Gospel of Wealth

John D. Rockefeller — Robber Baron or Industrial Statesman?

Roosevelt, Wilson, and the Trusts

Pragmatism and American Culture

The New Deal — Revolution or Evolution?

Industry-wide Collective Bargaining — Promise or Menace?

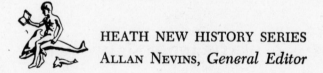

HEATH NEW HISTORY SERIES
ALLAN NEVINS, *General Editor*

The Causes of the
American Revolution

EDITED WITH AN INTRODUCTION BY
John C. Wahlke

Problems in American Civilization

READINGS SELECTED BY THE
DEPARTMENT OF AMERICAN STUDIES
AMHERST COLLEGE

D. C. HEATH AND COMPANY: Boston

Offices

Boston   New York   Chicago   Dallas
        Atlanta   San Francisco   London

INTRODUCTION

IT was not so very long ago that all Americans were taught that the American Revolution came about solely and simply because all colonists hated tyranny and loved freedom; because all colonists resented the denial by a foreign government of their right to share in governing themselves; and because all colonists, therefore, rising in heroic resistance to the government which oppressed them, determined to make of America an independent nation, founded on the principles of political liberty and equality. The persistence of such a simple and clear-cut picture of the revolutionary struggle is reflected in the widely-held belief that the chief point at issue between colonies and mother country was the rightness or wrongness of the principle, "taxation without representation is tyranny."

The labors of historians of the past two generations, however, have made it impossible to believe quite so surely that the Revolution was no more and no less than a conflict produced by verbal disagreements between a people united in the cause of freedom and a regime which refused to accept freedom as the necessary basis of all governments. The reappraisal of the colonial and revolutionary era, begun by such scholars as Charles M. Andrews, George Louis Beer, Herbert Levi Osgood, and others has made it clear that, to see selfless devotion of the patriots to political ideals as the sole cause of the Revolution might well be a national tradition, but it is hardly sound history. Significant facts which today seem obvious — for example, the extreme tardiness of the patriot leaders in formulating the demand for independence, or the apparent lack of unanimity among the colonists concerning what they wanted, why they wanted it, and how they proposed to get it — were long overlooked by the traditional explanations of why the revolutionists fought. Beginning in the 1890's, historians directed their attentions more closely to the revolutionary use of the political ideals of freedom and equality, of independence and self-government; they patiently considered the influence of such factors as economic interests, the accidental conjunctures of men and events, and the personal ambitions and prejudices of revolutionary leaders or members of Parliament; and they sought to discover all the possible logical connections between one step in the conflict and the next. As a result, there is today general agreement among historians that to understand why the Revolution was fought, one must do more than accept at face value the familiar political slogans and catch-words, that he must consider the actions and the motives of diverse individuals, groups, sections, and classes, and must be aware of the relation of the British-American conflict to British imperial problems and to larger problems of world affairs. There is no longer doubt that the causes of the

American Revolution were complex and deep seated.

However, the specific question, "What were the causes of the American Revolution?" is more than ever a major one, because the historians have failed to arrive at any answer upon which all can agree. Instead they present an array of contradictory and conflicting interpretations, from which the ordinary citizen must, somehow or other, choose or construct his own answer.

In any of these interpretations, a critical point of comparison is the extent to which the author believes the familiar revolutionary ideas and ideals to have been a major factor in producing the eventual war between Britons and colonists: it is possible to divide interpretations into two general categories, on the basis of their attitudes on this particular point. On the one hand, there are those writers who would de-emphasize the differences of political and constitutional ideas between the colonies and England, either by asserting that such opinions are only a product of some more basic economic or social factor, or by finding that, even though these different views constituted a genuine point of disagreement, the disagreement could readily have been overcome had it not been for conflicts of a different sort. Those who hold to such a viewpoint say, in effect, that what the colonists said and wrote about the rights of British citizens and the rights of men does not, *by itself,* offer any real clue as to why they fought.

On the other hand, there are writers who admit the complexity of causes of the Revolution, but insist that colonial ideas about democratic self-government were one of the most important causes of the Revolution and that the political views of the revolutionists cannot be *wholly* explained in terms of any direct, material interests or any inner logic of events.

The problem presented here, however, is much more specific than this difference in historical philosophy. Ever since Karl Marx first showed the way, most historians have been careful to take into account all economic aspects of their particular subject of interest. Many, of course, have gone so far as to say (though not often in precisely Marxist fashion) that the basic element in any historical situation is the economic one, and have gone on to apply this type of analysis to numerous specific cases. The American Revolution has not escaped such treatment. Rather, the economic interpretation has become one of the most prominent concerning that event. Writers like Charles Beard and Louis Hacker have offered cogent and complete arguments for it. In popular discussions about the nature or the causes of the Revolution, it will generally be found that those who profess to defend the honor of the revolutionary ideals regard as their principal enemy those who make even the least suggestion that the economic interests of the parties (especially of the colonists) played some part in the struggle. Economic interpretations of the Revolution have thus come to occupy a position of prominence not only in the eyes of their supporters, but in the eyes of opponents as well.

These readings, therefore, include important examples of two views: on the one hand, the view that economic conflicts between colonies and mother country were the paramount cause of the Revolution; on the other hand, the view that the Revolution was caused primarily by the differences in political ideas between colonists and Englishmen.

There is offered first a group of three selections relating solely to the arguments concerning the economic causation of the conflict. The first, by Louis M. Hacker, is the clearest possible presentation of the belief that it was the economic conflicts between colonial and British mercantile or industrial interests which led to the Revolutionary War. In the second selection, Charles M. Andrews gives his reasons for disagreeing with such an explanation, and in the third, John C. Miller presents a detailed examination of much the same material covered by Hacker, but comes to the conclusion that, while "underlying the resounding phrases and ideals of the American Revolution, there was a solid foundation of economic grievances," nevertheless,

it was the invasion of Americans' political rights by Parliament after the Peace of Paris which precipitated the struggle . . . and inspired the ideals and slogans of the American Revolution.

In the second group of readings, attention is given to the course of events between 1764 and 1776, rather than to the general economic background of the period. Carl Becker's brilliant re-creation of the period through the eyes of Jeremiah Wynkoop and his father-in-law, Nicholas Van Schoickendinck, offers persuasive argument that the political beliefs of at least one of these two fictional participants was neither wholly nor logically related to his economic and class interests; the implication is clear that such political ideas were vital causes of the conflict. In the next selection, by John C. Miller, the reader is offered a detailed account of the climactic months which culminated in the Declaration of Independence. A thorough understanding of this final crisis is of crucial importance, in as much as it was only in this period that the principles and ideals of

the Revolutionary cause took the form in which they have been handed down to later generations of Americans.

The selection by Claude H. Van Tyne is devoted to an examination of the political and constitutional points at issue between the colonies and the mother country. It is Van Tyne's contention that disagreement upon basic political ideas, resulting in clashing interpretations of the proper nature of the British constitution, made it impossible for the colonies to remain within the Empire unless one or the other of the disputants should surrender on these matters of principle.

The next group of selections offers two further interpretations of the revolutionary period in more general terms. Lawrence Henry Gipson's argument that the Revolution was essentially a product of the world struggle for empire can hardly be said to offer total support to either the political or the economic interpretation, as developed in this volume. Gipson's contention that further subordination to the Empire was against the material interests of major segments of the American community after 1763 implies that those material interests were much more basic motivations of the colonists than were their political and constitutional beliefs; his contention that the war with France bred major changes in British colonial policy, however, undermines one of the central features of the economic interpretation — that British policy remained mercantilist, dictated by British capitalist interests, right down to 1776. The bearing of the companion selection, by James Truslow Adams, is much the same. Adams argues that the interests and political ideals of merchants were basically different from those of the radicals in the colonies. He thus raises, for the economic interpretation, the serious question: How does the economic conflict between British and colonial capitalists account for the discontent of frontiersmen, artisans, and other radicals and to what extent was the Revolution the work of these radicals? For the opposite view, the question raised by Adams is: Can the political and constitutional views of the colonists be understood only in the light of the social background and the class interests of the various segments of the American people?

The readings conclude with Peter H. Odegard's review of Philip Davidson's book, *Propaganda and the American Revolution*. In view of present-day fears concerning propaganda and the manipulation of opinion, no consideration of the American Revolution is complete if it does not take into account the extent to which Revolutionary political ideas were propagandistic in nature. The label, "propaganda," suggests to many readers that the ideas so labelled must necessarily be untrue, or at least irrelevant to the real thought and interests of the propagandists. Odegard's article offers reasons for rejecting such a belief, and for accepting the revolutionary ideals in good faith in spite of their so-called propaganda value.

While the major problem thus presented is one of broad historical interpretation, it is impossible to weigh the relative significance of political ideas and economic interests without first facing a number of essentially factual subsidiary questions, upon which the authors disagree at many points. One such question involves the nature of British colonial policy after 1763: Did the British government change its policy at that time, thus producing grievances which would not have arisen otherwise, or did it continue a mercantilist policy which intensified old grievances? Related to this is the question: To what extent were the colonists themselves aware of specifically economic grievances, and to what extent did they express them? What grievances did the colonists have, if not primarily economic ones? A very critical question concerns the role of the different sections and classes in the colonies: What grievances and what political ideas did artisans and small farmers have in common with merchants, or frontiersmen with city-dwellers, and where did the interests and ideas of these groups diverge from one another? Is it possible to determine which actions were the work of merchants, which the work of radicals, and which the results of their joint efforts? If so, how did those actions interrelate to cause a revolution?

Only after considering such questions as these will the reader be able to decide whether he thinks the Revolution came about because of the devotion of some or all colonists to political and constitutional ideals, or because the economic interests of some or all colonists could be served, in the long run, only by political independence from England. It need hardly be said that the formulation of an intelligent opinion on this particular problem should yield something much more valuable than mere intellectual exercise. A study of the causes of the American Revolution, since it demands a questioning of the function of democratic ideals in the founding of the American nation, necessarily demands further questioning of the function of those same ideals in our own time. An understanding of the relationship of the ideals of 1776 to the economic and social situation of the revolutionary period will contribute to a better understanding of the possible utility of those ideals in solving ideological and interest conflicts within the American community today. And an understanding of the relationship of the interests and ideals of 1776 to the constitution of the 18th-century British Empire will certainly offer some basis for deciding what should be America's role in the 20th-century world-community of nations.

[NOTE: The statements on page xii are quoted, with the permission of the publishers, from the following sources: Charles M. Andrews, "The American Revolution: An Interpretation," *American Historical Review*, XXXI (January, 1926), 230; Louis M. Hacker, "The First American Revolution," *Columbia University Quarterly*, XXVII, No. 3 (September, 1935), 290; John C. Miller, *Triumph of Freedom, 1775–1783* (Boston: Little, Brown and Company, 1948), p. 687; James Blaine Walker, *The Epic of American Industry* (New York: Harper and Brothers, 1949), p. xi; Claude H. Van Tyne, *The Causes of the War of Independence* (New York: Houghton Mifflin Company, 1922), p. 237.]

CONTENTS

The Clash of Issues

"Primarily, the American Revolution was a political and constitutional movement and only secondarily one that was either financial, commercial, or social. At bottom the fundamental issue was the political independence of the colonies, and in the last analysis the conflict lay between the British Parliament and the colonial assemblies. . . ."

— Charles M. Andrews

"The struggle was not over high-sounding political and constitutional concepts: over the power of taxation and, in the final analysis, over natural rights: but over colonial manufacturing, wild lands and furs, sugar, wine, tea and currency, all of which meant, simply, the survival or collapse of English merchant capitalism within the imperial-colonial framework of the mercantilist system."

— Louis M. Hacker

"The American Revolution was, as Thomas Paine said, the accomplishment of an age — the fruition of eighteenth-century liberalism."

— John C. Miller

"In seeking liberty to trade we were impelled to secure political freedom. The winning of the Revolution and the adoption of the Constitution had their roots in our economic necessities."

— James Blaine Walker

". . . differences in ideals were as important causes of a breaking-up of the empire as more concrete matters like oppressive taxation. . . . There was no ruinous material damage to America in the attempted taxation, but as John Dickinson said, 'A free people can never be too quick in observing nor too firm in opposing the beginnings of alteration either in form or reality, respecting institutions formed for their security. . . .'"

— Claude H. Van Tyne

Louis M. Hacker:

THE FIRST AMERICAN REVOLUTION

THAT America has had a revolutionary past is, by this time, common knowledge; but that the first American Revolution, the war of independence against England, in quite every significant particular conformed to the revolutionary outlines of those better-known uprisings, the French Revolution and the Russian Revolution, is not generally understood. It is difficult to find disinterested students who are willing to contend that the French Revolution and the Russian Revolution could have been averted; for it must be apparent, given the character of the existing productive forces and the economic and social relations growing out of them, the shaping class antagonisms, and the onset of crisis, that the revolutionary challenge to authority on the part of the French bourgeoisie in one instance and of the Russian proletariat in the other was as inevitable as the normal progression of human life from birth to death. In both France and Russia, continued existence within the restricting forms of a declining productive system had become impossible; in each case, matters had been brought to a head within a brief and crowded interval by desperate efforts on the part of the ruling classes to continue in control of the corporate agencies of privilege; in each, the revolt was undertaken by underprivileged classes who, forming themselves into extra-legal groups, swept aside the by then dead hand of prerogative authority and erected revolutionary governments.

Such, also, were the broad outlines of the revolutionary process in colonial America, beginning with the last third of the eighteenth century: the general characteristics of contradiction, repression, crisis and thrust for power all were present. All these things we know: there are any number of American scholars who can without difficulty tick off the titles of virtually hundreds of monographs and learned articles that in detail support such an interpretation. And yet, it is one of the curiosities of American scholarship that no effort has been made to unite all these generally accepted facts into a coherent pattern.

Many historians, today, in trying to plumb the mystery of the American Revolution, seem to be quite as ingenuous in their approach as Parson Weems, the redoubtable creator of the Washingtonian myth. To the good preacher the reason for American revolt was altogether simple: the colonies were being plundered to take care of the royal poor relations and to feed the insatiable appetites of the ministers surrounding the English throne. Such an explanation, by personalizing the oppressive forces, undoubtedly serves an important patriotic function when all the issues of the struggle have not been yet resolved, but obviously it will not do long after passions have cooled. Incredible as it may seem, this

Reprinted from *Columbia University Quarterly,* Volume XXVII, Number 3, Part 1 (September, 1935). Copyright 1935 by Columbia University Press.

explanation has not altogether disappeared from history books, although, of course, its present-day guise is surrounded perhaps with an air of greater thoughtfulness. Thus, Professor Channing, writing in 1909, could say that the issue was not forced by the patriots of 1763–1775: "That was the work of selfish placemen in England, whose horizon was bounded by the narrow seas of their own island, and of over-zealous and stubborn officials in America, whose thoughts were ever intent upon places and pensions — Townshend, Hillsborough, and Lord North in England; Hutchinson, Dudingston and Tryon in America."

Also, to see the Revolution simply as a struggle for democratic rights in the political sphere: to build the whole theory of the Revolution around the slogan "No Taxation Without Representation" and to consider it merely as a continuation of "the Englishman's long struggle for political liberty," in the face of the almost immediate repeal by Parliament of the Stamp Tax Act and the Townshend duties and despite the fact that in the colonies themselves (as in England) the great mass of the adult population was disfranchised anyway: this is to make confusion only worse confounded. Nor is it possible to regard the struggle as arising out of a change in English colonial policy: that, beginning with 1763, the doctrine of mercantilism, with its more or less casual relations between mother country and dependencies, was replaced by the more modern concept of imperialism, under which the colonies were to be closely integrated into the political life of the whole empire. We are to believe (at least upon the authority of Professor Van Tyne) that a race of stubborn imperial patriots, originating in the landed classes entirely, had suddenly come into control of affairs with the termination of the Seven Years' War and was bent upon consolidating the empire in the interests of the greater glory of England, the opposition of the home merchant classes to the contrary notwithstanding.

At the basis of these various beliefs is the supposition that if only wiser heads had been guiding the English ship of state, if a beneficent statesmanship and not embittered partisanship had prevailed — if only Burke, Barré and a well Chatham had been the directors of the empire's destinies! — then Americans today, like all good British subjects, would be celebrating the King's Jubilee along with Canadians, Jamaicans and Fiji Islanders. For had not the great Whig leaders continuously pleaded for conciliation: for an end to colonial coercion, for withdrawal of troops, for the abandonment of all those policies whose only effect was to convert contented colonials into disloyal and plotting subjects? In short, accommodation was possible. (This thought, like a minor theme, runs through the writings of all modern American scholars. So, Professor Andrews declares: "We are driven to believe that a little more yielding, a little more of the spirit of friendliness and compromise, and a little less of British ignorance, stubbornness and prejudice would have calmed the troubled waters and stilled the storm that was brewing.") Accommodation was possible: the dispute about trade was a minor matter, the heated controversy over taxation was quickly adjusted in America's favor, the troops were insignificant irritants and could quickly have been removed: for, in effect, the English Whigs were right in assuming that mercantilism could work forever — if there could be only a fair degree of give and take. We shall see — obviously the Revolution can have no meaning otherwise — that the break took place not because of the inauguration by England of a new policy but because the sharpening of the contradictions that lay at the heart of mercantilism had to tear asunder the imperial-colonial relations.

Finally, scholars find refuge in an obscurantism that is difficult to penetrate; and there is nothing more surprising than to see Professor Andrews, who has done so much to clarify the nature of the commercial relations existing between England and its colonies, adopting such a position. The following is Professor Andrews' argument. For one hundred and fifty years, from the very hour of settlement itself, mother country and colonies had been growing farther and farther apart psychologically and institutionally. England was "an old, well-settled, highly organized land"; its social and economic life had hardened into iron-bound molds; its ruling class, seated on its great estates and in firm possession of all the citadels of privilege, was guided by "rigid and sinister ideas of power and government." The colonies, on the other hand, were youthful, growing, and filled with "a frontier people instinct with individualism and possessed of but a rudimentary sense of obligation and duty." Thus, it really was the old, old struggle between aristocracy and democracy, between settled areas, with an ancient culture and a caste tradition, and the frontier with a fluid institutional life and a passionate belief in egalitarianism. The magical concept of the frontier, it seems, will explain everything to American historians. What if class divisions were as sharply drawn in the colonies as in England, that the colonial merchants and their legal spokesmen were as contemptuous of "mobsters" as were their English counterparts, that colonial planters settled on their broad acres in Virginia, Maryland and South Carolina lived as much in the aristocratic tradition as noble lords with estates in Surrey and Kent? All this, apparently, is irrelevant. The frontier made Americans free and out of this individualism was engendered a spirit of liberty.

In the face of these conflicting and implausible theories of learned scholars, bewilderment on the part of the uninformed is only natural. Unless we are prepared to start out with the premise that the economic and social relations flowing out of the prevailing system of the day, that is to say, mercantilism, no longer could be maintained, then the whole history of the critical period that preceded the American Revolution is simply unintelligible. And if the past does not make sense, then we must consign its study over to the pure and simple antiquarians. But because the past has a clear and inevitable logic, our study of this period in America's development is of the greatest contemporary significance because we, today, living as we do also in an era of productive decline, class oppressions and approaching crisis, have much to learn from the ways employed by American patriots of an earlier time in the resolution of their perplexities.

II

The economic program the rulers of England adopted following the successful termination of the Puritan Revolution of 1641–49 (all the gains of the Revolution were finally consolidated with the establishment of the constitutional monarchy in 1689) we have come to call mercantilism. What mercantilism was, simply, was a policy to assure the continued advance of the English merchant, or pre-industrial, capitalism, once the restrictive ties of the absolute and mediaeval state had been cast off. In this sense, therefore, mercantilism had two faces: at home it utilized the agency of the state to strengthen the position of commercial enterprisers in trade, manufacturing and agriculture; and abroad, particularly in the colonial relations, it from the beginning attached the oversea possessions in a subordinate capacity to the economy of the mother country. We shall not understand the character of the American crisis of 1763–1775 unless we are prepared to hold ever in mind the fact that every imperial administrative program, whether in the economic or political realms, was designed to further this end: to utilize the colonies as an economic appanage of the mother country. That the English from the very beginning were fully conscious of the nature of this relationship, there is ample evidence. Thus, as early as 1726, a member of the Board of Trade wrote:

Every act of a dependent provincial government ought therefore to terminate in the advantage of the mother state unto whom it owes its being and protection in all its valuable privileges. Hence it follows that all advantageous projects or commercial gains in any colony which are truly prejudicial to and inconsistent with the interests of the mother state must be understood to be illegal and the practice of them unwarrantable, because they contradict the end for which the colony had a being and are incompatible with the terms on which the people claim both privileges and protection. . . . For such is the end of the colonies, and if this use cannot be made of them it will be much better for the state to be without them.

It is apparent, therefore, that mercantilism was more than a monetary policy, as is so commonly believed. It is true that mercantilism did place a high value on a favorable balance of trade and as a result sought to encourage a flow of the precious metals into the home country.

But there was no confusion in the minds of merchant capitalists of the day as to the real nature of wealth, they did not see it, that is to say, as merely money stocks but also as ownership of the means of production. Money was not unprofitably employed in the foreign trade even if exports exceeded imports; for balances could be converted into means for the acquisition of the agencies of production, notably oversea lands, and in this way the stimulation of further raw materials encouraged. Under the system of imperial-colonial relations there took place a constant flow of English capital into the staple-producing colonies. Where mercantilism broke down, as we shall see, was in the fact that these investments were made only in land and not in manufacturing. Had the policy permitted the expansion of English capitalist enterprise into colonial large-scale manufacturing, the colonial tie would never have been sundered; at any rate, certainly not in 1776.

At home in England, the mercantilist policy was developed along the following lines: in the interests of commercial agriculture, the process of enclosure was renewed on the one hand and the Corn Laws were revived and strengthened on the other to assure the country of the continuance of an adequate fiber and food supply; in the interests of industry, the state bent every energy to assure a steady flow of raw materials, protect the domestic market, and prescribe standards of quality so that competition in oversea markets with foreign producers could be successfully overcome; in the interests of commerce, the carrying trade was made a national monopoly through the agency of the Navigation Acts. With the measures taken to support English agriculture, we have no immediate concern here; but English policy in the fields of industry and commerce merits some examination.

Throughout the whole period in which the mercantilist theory was the guide to state conduct, Parliament was constantly exercising itself on behalf of the manufacturing interest. It discouraged the importation of foreign finished goods, of course, through the imposition of high duties and embargoes; it removed duties on foreign raw materials; it forbade the exportation of wool; and it controlled standards of quality, so that as regards the woolen industry alone, by the end of the eighteenth century, there were on the statute books some three hundred pieces of legislation which laid down rules for the maintenance of fineness of cloth, dimensions, composition of raw materials entering into fabrics, and the like. But even more important, Parliament and its administrative agencies granted enterprisers fiscal immunities, paid bounties, prevented the emigration of skilled workers, placed embargoes on the exports of tools, by regulation compelled the compulsory wearing of home-produced textiles, and finally, seriously circumscribed the processes by which English capital might be exported out of the country into any fields other than the production of raw materials.

As regards encouragement of trade, the devices employed by the English government are well known. The Navigation System, reinaugurated in 1650, had as its initial purpose the wresting of sea power away from the Dutch; but its subsequent extensions were openly designed to shut down English ports to foreign ships. The intention behind the policy was the building up of the English merchant marine and the creation of a national monopoly of the carrying trade, still that chief source of profit of merchant capitalist enterprise.

III

In the interests of English merchant capitalism, control over the economic life of the colonies was even more closely supervised. It has only too frequently been assumed that English colonial policy underwent a marked transformation in the middle of the eighteenth century and that this change was responsible for the onset of the crisis of 1763–75. Whereas, up to about the middle of the eighteenth century, Englishmen looked upon the colonies merely as sources for the production of raw materials, after that period they regarded them chiefly as markets for finished goods; and the desire to extend the market led to the acquisition of Canada and the western lands, and therefore the creation of that whole imperial administrative machinery of taxation, the quartering of troops, and the like, which inevitably brought on the break. A moment's reflection must indicate the inadequacy of this theory. Commercial intercourse between home country and colonies was possible only on the basis of the steady flow of goods and services between the two; and if the colonies were to be encouraged to sell their raw materials in the home country it was imperative that they be created into open markets for the absorption of English finished goods and the services of English ship-owners, merchants and financiers. The balance of payments was largely to be maintained by the colonial export of sugar, tobacco, indigo, dyewoods, logwoods and naval stores to England and the colonial import from England of drygoods and hardware as visible items. Invisible items, to the credit of English merchant capitalism, were to be freights, brokerage, insurance, commissions, profits and interest on borrowings. But what if the flow of goods and services from the colonies did not equal the flow of goods and services to the colonies? What was to be the utilization of the surpluses to the credit of the mother country? For sooner or later, in all imperial-colonial relations, the tendency for colonial debits is to outstrip credits: this was particularly true under mercantilism where the mother country was virtually the only source of finished goods and the principal outlet for raw materials.

The only factor that distinguished mercantilist imperial-colonial relations from modern-day imperialist imperial-colonial relations was the utilization of the capital surpluses. Under mercantilism, the colonies were pressed to make returns on unfavorable balances in specie and when specie was not constantly available (as it usually was not), the creditor home country was compelled to invest its surpluses in the colonies in land and land operations. Under imperialism, the investment of surpluses is in all types of capital goods: in land of course, but with an accelerating tempo in factories, public utilities, means of transportation and the like. In other words, under mercantilism the colonies could never look forward to duplicating the advancing industrial economy of the mother country, for native capital accumulations or foreign capital surpluses could not be employed in manufacturing but always in agricultural and trading operations; under imperialism, industrial duplication sooner or later becomes the prime characteristic, so that we see today, for example, British Indians, utilizing English capital, engaged in the manufacture of cotton textiles to compete with English textiles in the Far Eastern market.

The American colonies, therefore, from the very beginning, were attached to the English leading string; and it was their economic function to produce raw materials that England needed and to consume (but not manufacture themselves) English finished goods. The development of forms of enterprise calculated to enter into competition with English capitalism was seriously frowned upon, efforts were made to check them, and when everything else failed rigorous measures aiming at suppression were adopted.

The whole purpose of the Acts of Trade and Navigation was this design to keep in balance the economic relations between mother country and colonies; and all the administrative devices utilized had the same function in the social and legal spheres. Outstanding among the methods employed to assure the flow of colonial raw materials into the English market was that known as the enumeration of articles, as a result of which certain commodities might be exported only to England. In the act of 1660, the first list of enumerated articles contained sugar, tobacco, ginger, cotton-wool and fustic and other dyewoods; in an act of 1706, rice, naval stores, hemp, masts and yards were added to the list; in 1722, copper ore and beaver and other furs were included; in 1733, molasses was listed; and in 1764, whale fins, hides, iron, lumber, raw silk and potash and pearl ashes were enumerated.

On a second front, control over the colonial economy was pressed through prohibitions against the establishment of local manufactures. This had two effects: it prevented English capital surpluses from being invested in the colonies in large-scale industry, diverting them largely into land speculation and commercial agriculture; and it similarly prevented colonial surpluses from finding outlets in industrial enterprise, diverting them into commercial, or trading, activities. The placing of insuperable obstacles in the way of the employment of capital in the expansive field of colonial manufactures was undoubtedly the outstanding reason for breakdown in the imperial-colonial relations and the bringing on of the revolutionary crisis that led to the War of Independence. By specific enactment, in 1699, Parliament sought to check the development of a colonial woolen industry by forbidding the entrance of colonial wool, woolen yarn and woolen manufactures into foreign or intercolonial commerce. In 1732, similar action was taken in the case of the growing colonial hat-making industry by preventing the exportation of hats out of the separate colonies and by restricting colonial hat makers to two apprentices. In 1750, colonials were denied the right to extend the manufacture of wrought iron, by being forbidden to erect new slitting and rolling mills, plating forges and steel furnaces.

It has been generally stated that these prohibitions were uniformly disregarded and that the reasons why large-scale manufacturing did not flourish in the colonies were to be found elsewhere. There are plain evidences why we may assume that manufacturing was retarded in the colonies exactly because of the operations of the mercantilist prohibition. Thus, at the very time in England when domestic manufacturing was rapidly being converted into the factory system, and great advances were being made in the perfection of machinery exactly because the existence of a growing market was demanding more efficient methods of production, in the colonies methods of production remained at a hopelessly backward level because of the impossibility of setting up large workshops without running foul of the law. Again, the great expansion of the colonial crude iron industry and its outstripping of the English industry in less than half

a century points to the advanced development of colonial merchant capitalism. Also, the heavy investments made by colonials in the carrying trade, and in commercial enterprise generally, during the greater part of the eighteenth century, indicates that there was no dearth of colonial capital accumulations.

Nor was there the absence of a colonial market. With the opening of the eighteenth century the population of America had begun to increase by leaps and bounds, doubling itself every generation. Coastal America presented all the aspects of a well-established and secure society. The British controlled the seaboard region in an unbroken stretch from Maine to Florida and in it improved areas were virtually continuous; the line of the wilderness was steadily being pushed back to the crest of the Appalachians; there were adequate facilities for communication and intelligence. The countryside, in every section of the domain, was dotted with pleasant farmhouses whose occupants had long ago learned to enjoy many of the amenities and conveniences of a settled civilization. Everything was ready for the coming of industrialism; everything, that is, but a fluid and free capital supply, and this waited on the release of American merchant capitalism from the constricting limitations of English mercantilist policy.

IV

The economy of the Southern continental colonies was based on the commercial production of a number of raw materials, or staples, vital to the continuance of merchant capitalism in England. These were tobacco, rice, furs, naval stores and indigo. The most important of these, of course, was tobacco and, as we have seen, the English monopolized the tobacco trade by requiring that the whole Southern crop be shipped only to English ports. Throughout the eighteenth century, as the Southern tobacco crop grew larger and larger, the unit price in London tended to drop periodically below the cost of production; in addition, capital costs of plantation operation mounted due to the high cost of labor (the price of indentured servants and more particularly that of slaves went up while their productivity remained constant), the exhaustion of the soil in the older regions, and the necessity on the part of the planters to buy new lands to which they could be ready to transfer their activities when the older areas no longer were economically cultivatable. There were other charges against operations that did not fall with the unit price of tobacco but tended to remain constant or indeed increased: freight costs, insurance, merchants' commissions and profits (for handling the crop and purchasing the planters' necessaries), and interest on borrowings: and all these items were paid in England in pounds sterling.

Thus, virtually from the beginning, the plantation system was conducted on a narrow margin of profit which, by the middle of the eighteenth century, probably had contracted almost to the vanishing point. What sustained the Southern plantation economy? It was nothing else than the presence of easily preempted lands in the wilderness areas west of the regions of cultivation which planters were able to buy up for speculative purposes. The ability of planters to make a profit (not on the cultivation of their staples but in their rôle as speculative landlords) furnished the incentive for the flow of short-term capital from England into the Southern colonies for the financing of the planting, cultivating, harvesting, and shipping of their crops, the purchase of their servants and slaves,

and the satisfaction of their personal and household needs. And short-term borrowings were converted into long-term indebtedness by the placing of mortgages on plantations and slaves. When these profits from speculative land operations threatened to disappear the flow of English credit ceased: and Southern planters were confronted by wholesale bankruptcy.

Because the wild lands of the frontier areas were so important to the maintenance of the stability of the Southern planting economy, Southern merchant capitalism was constantly preoccupied with them. The west was not opened up by the hardy frontiersman; it was opened up by the land speculator who preceded even the Daniel Boones of the wilderness. When the young Washington surveyed the lands around the waters of the upper Potomac in 1748 he was doing so as the representative of a great colonial landlord and as the scion of a rich landowning family; and when he bought up soldier bounty claims in the decade following he was only pursuing the same line of interest already marked out by the Fairfaxes, the Lees, and the Mercers.

But the English (and the Scotch, in this case) had also learned to regard with more than a curious interest these wild lands of the west: they saw in them opportunities for profits from the fur trade and from the speculative exploitation of the region by their own capitalist enterprise. It was at this point that English and American merchant capitalism came into conflict and when, as a result of the promulgation of the Proclamation Line of 1763 and the Quebec Act of 1774, the western lands were virtually closed to colonial enterprising, Southern merchant capitalism began to totter on its throne. Without the subsidiary activity of land speculation, the planting economy could not continue solvent; there is no cause for wonder therefore that Southern planters were among the first to swell the ranks of the colonial revolutionary host.

Nothing indicates more completely the debtor position of Southern commercial agriculture than the mounting burden of debt and the almost continuous attention devoted by Southern assemblies to cheapmoney measures. At the outbreak of the Revolution it was not unlikely that the American colonies were indebted to English merchant capitalists to the extent of fully £5,000,000, of which at least fivesixths had been incurred by the Southern planters. These bore heavy interest charges, and funds for short-term operations and for long-term renewals were becoming increasingly difficult to obtain as English creditors took alarm after 1763. I. S. Harrell, whose excellent monograph[1] plainly reveals the economic basis of revolutionary crisis and struggle in the most important Southern colony, Virginia, sums up the situation in these words: "With their plantations, slaves, and sometimes household furniture hypothecated, the planters were in an almost inextricable position in 1775."

V

The Northern economy in its capitalist relations was based chiefly not on agriculture, as in the case of the South, but on trade. The Northern colonies directly produced little of those staples that England required: the grains, provisions and work animals of New England and New York and Pennsylvania could not be permitted to enter England lest they disorganize the home commercial agricultural industry; and the fishing catches of the New England fishing fleets competed

with the English fishery industry operating in the North Sea and off the Newfoundland coast. The Northern colonies, of course, were a source for lumber, naval stores, furs, whale products and iron, and these England sorely needed to maintain her independence of European supplies. By bounties, the relaxing of trade restrictions, and the granting of favored positions in the home market, England sought to encourage these industries, partly because it required these staples and partly to divert Northern capital from expanding further into shipbuilding, shipping and manufacturing. But the policy yielded no really successful results. The advance of population into frontier zones cut down the field of operations of the fur trade; the Northern merchants found more profitable outlets for their lumber in the West Indian sugar islands and in the Spanish and Portuguese wine islands off the African coast; although the production of crude iron received a great stimulus as a result of English encouragement, most of the pigs and bars came to be absorbed in the colonies themselves so that the export of iron to England was disappointing; while the production of naval stores, despite a consistent program of bounties launched upon by England as early as 1706, never took hold in the Northern colonies and therefore the plan of the Board of Trade to keep Northern merchant capitalism entirely dependent upon England completely failed.

The Northern colonies, therefore, produced little for direct export to England to permit them to pay their balances; for balances there were to be paid despite the household manufacturing of textiles and the fabrication of iron goods. They were buying increasing quantities of English drygoods, hardware and house furnishings, and were thus heavy debtors

[1] *Loyalism in Virginia* (Durham, N. C., 1926).

on visible account (and even on invisible items, although they were using their own services of shipping, commercial exchanges and the like) in the direct trade. Also — and this is an economic factor of the utmost significance — the Northern colonies never, to any appreciable extent, presented important opportunities for English capital investment. As we have seen, the English capital stake was largely in the South: only to a very slight degree was any of it to be found in the North. The result was the imperative necessity for the Northern colonies to develop returns in order to obtain specie and bills of exchange with which to balance payments in England.

The most important of these was trade (and the subsidiary industries growing out of trade) with areas outside of England. Northern merchants and shipowners opened up regular markets in New-foundland and Nova Scotia for their fishing tackle, salt, provisions and rum; they established a constant and ever-growing commercial intercourse with the wine islands of the Canaries and Madeira, from which they bought their light and fortified wines direct instead of by way of England and to which they sold barrel staves, foodstuffs and live animals; they sold fish to Spain, Portugal, and Italy; their ports to a measurable extent during the eighteenth century (and in this way they competed directly with the English shipping fleets plying between England and the Southern colonies) acted as entrepôts for the transshipment of Southern staples — tobacco, hardwoods and dyewoods, indigo — to England and of rice to Southern Europe.

The trade with the West Indian sugar islands — as well as the traffic in Negro slaves and the manufacture of rum, which grew out of it — became the cornerstone of the Northern colonial capitalist economy. Northern merchants, loading their small swift ships with all those necessaries the sugar planters of the West Indies were economically unable to produce — work animals for their mills; lumber for houses and outbuildings; staves, heads and hoops for barrels; flour and salted provisions for their tables; and low-grade fish for their slaves — made regular runs from Salem, Boston, Bristol, Newport, New York and Philadelphia originally to the British islands of Barbados, the Leeward Islands and Jamaica, and then increasingly to the French, Spanish, Dutch and Danish islands and settlements dotting the Caribbean. Here they acquired in return specie for the payment of their English balances, indigo, cotton, ginger, allspice and dyewoods for transshipment to England and, above all, sugar and molasses for conversion into rum in the distilleries of Massachusetts and Rhode Island. It was this wondrous alcoholic beverage that served as the basis of the intercourse between the Northern colonies and the African coast: and in return the Northern traders picked up ivory, gums and beeswax and, most important of all, Negro slaves which were again carried to the sugar islands on that famous Middle Passage to furnish the labor supply without which the sugar plantation economy could not survive.

The freights, commissions and profits earned as a result of the successful conduct of trading enterprise thus furnished important sources of return through which Northern merchant capitalists obtained specie and foreign bills of exchange with which to pay English balances. Shipbuilding, with New England and later Philadelphia as the leading centers, was another source. Northern ships were sold for use in the intercolonial trade and in the local trades of the West Indies and the wine islands; also ships were frequently sold in England and Southern Europe after the completion of voyages. Still another source of return was the colonial fisheries. Northern fishermen, operating in fishing craft and whalers owned by colonial merchant capitalists, fished and hunted the waters off the New England coast and increasingly penetrated northward into the Newfoundland Banks.

Apparently, however, despite the complexity of all this activity still other means of obtaining remittances had to be developed: and these Northern merchant capitalists soon found in three illegal forms of enterprise — piracy, smuggling generally, and particularly the illicit sugar and molasses trade with the foreign West Indian islands.

It is not generally appreciated to what extent piracy — at least up to the end of the seventeenth century — played a significant rôle in maintaining the merchant capitalism of the Northern colonies. English and colonial pirates, fitted out in the ports of Boston, Newport, New York and Philadelphia and backed financially by reputable merchants, preyed on the Spanish fleets of the Caribbean and even boldly fared out into the Red Sea and the Indian Ocean to terrorize ships engaged in the East Indies trade; and with their ships heavily laden with plate, drygoods and spices, they put back into colonial ports where they sold their loot and divided their profits with the merchants who had financed them. It is impossible, of course, to estimate the size of this traffic; that it was great every evidence indicates. Curtis P. Nettels cites reports that single pirate ships frequently brought in cargoes valued at between £50,000 and £200,000; that New York province alone obtained £100,000 in treasure yearly from the illicit traffic; and

that the greater supply of specie in the colonies before 1700 than after (after that date England began its successful war of extermination against the seafaring marauders) undoubtedly was due to the open support of piratical expeditions and the gains obtained thereby by some of the wisest mercantile heads in the Northern towns.[2]

Smuggling also contributed its share to swell the remittances the Northern merchants so badly needed. Smuggling traffic could be carried on in a number of directions. In the first place, there was the illegal direct intercourse between the colonies and European countries in the expanding list of enumerated articles; and in the second place, ships on the home-bound voyages from Europe or from the West Indies brought large supplies of drygoods, silk, cocoa and brandies into the American colonies without having declared them at English ports and paid the duties. Most important of all, of course, was the trade with the foreign West Indian sugar islands which was rendered illegal, after 1733, as a result of the imposition by the Molasses Act of prohibitive duties on the importation into the colonies of foreign sugar, molasses and rum. It is imperative that something be said of the productive system and the social and economic relations prevailing in the sugar islands, for just as the western lands constituted the Achilles heel of the Southern planting economy so the trade with the sugar islands — and notably that with the foreign islands — was the highly vulnerable

[2] See his *The Money Supply of the American Colonies Before 1720* (Madison, Wis., 1934), one of the truly outstanding monographs in American colonial history. The writer is deeply indebted to Professor Nettels, and much of his own analysis of the money relations existing between mother country and colonies follows this pioneer work.

point in Northern commercial economy. When England, beginning with 1763, struck at these two vital and exposed centers, it immediately threatened the very existence of colonial merchant capitalism.

VI

By the opening of the second third of the eighteenth century, the English sugar planters of the West Indies were beginning to find themselves hard pressed, in the great colonial sugar market, by the steadily growing competition of the foreign sugar planters in the islands and settlements owned by the French, Spanish, Dutch and Danes. The British sugar planters occupied a unique position in the imperial-colonial sphere. Favored from the very beginning by the tender solicitude of English imperial officialdom, supported in all their extravagant demands for protection by the great English merchant capitalist interest allied with and dependent upon them, in time represented in Parliament itself by what today we would call a sugar bloc, the plantation lords of Barbados, the Leeward Islands and Jamaica exerted an influence on British colonial policy that, in the words of Professor Andrews, "was probably greater than even that of politics, war and religion." The reasons for this are not difficult to find. Sugar, more so even than tobacco, was the great oversea staple of the eighteenth-century world; it was a household necessary, it had a constant and growing market everywhere in Western Europe, it was the basis for the flourishing of a ramified English commercial industry made up of carriers, commission men, factors, financiers, processors and distributors. Also, sugar was converted into molasses which in turn was distilled into rum; and it was rum that was the very heart of the unholy

slave traffic and the unsavory Indian trade. Small wonder, therefore, that sugar cultivation attracted at once the concentrated attention of English merchant capitalism: and by the time Adam Smith was writing English capitalism had succeeded in building up in the islands plantations with a capital worth of fully £60,000,000 – a gigantic sum even in our modern imperialist age. Of this amount, at least half continued to remain the stake of home English investors in long-term (land titles and mortgages) and short-term investments. When it is recalled that in the whole of the North American continental colonies the English capitalist stake at most was only one-sixth as great, the reason for the favoring of the sugar colonies as against the Northern commercial colonies, after 1763, is revealed in a single illuminating flash.

By the second third of the eighteenth century it was everywhere being admitted that the English sugar planting economy was being uneconomically operated.[3] Plantations were large and were worked by inefficient slave labor and primitive methods; affairs of business were in the hands of paid clerks; no attention was paid to the restoration of the soil's fertility; the single crop was planted year in and year out without thought to the state of the market and mounting operating costs; and the whole system was stripped of its productive capital to sustain in idleness and luxury an absentee owning class. It was the dream of every British West Indian to flee from his tropical estate and settle in England, where he could buy a country property and a seat in Parliament and

[3] See L. J. Ragatz's *The Fall of the Planter Class in the British Caribbean, 1763–83* (New York, 1928); and F. W. Pitman's *Development of the British West Indies, 1700–63* (New Haven, 1917).

play the English country gentleman. This was generally realized: and by the early 1770's more than seventy plantation lords sat for country boroughs in the English Parliament and were therefore in a position to fight savagely all efforts at survival on the part of Northern colonial merchant capitalism.

This was all very well as long as nothing appeared to endanger the sugar monopoly of the English planters. But with the third decade of the eighteenth century, following the establishment of peace, such rivals appeared in the shape of foreign planters, notably the French: and the British planting interest was being threatened. The foreign planters clearly were at an advantage: their lands were newer and therefore more productive; ownership-operation, on the basis of small holdings, was the rule, with therefore more efficient methods and lower operating and capital costs; and diversification was practiced, the coffee crop of some of the islands often exceeding the sugar crop. These factors, growing out of their superior economy, permitted the French and other foreign sugar planters to undersell the British. There were other reasons, implicit in the English mercantilist scheme, which strengthened further their command of the market; British sugar was compelled to pay a heavy export tax (4½ per cent) at the island ports; also, it was an enumerated commodity and could be sold only to England or its colonies; on the other hand, foreign sugar was free of imposts and enjoyed lower marketing costs as a result of its ability to reach oversea markets directly.

All this Englishmen and colonials saw. Adam Smith referred to the "superiority" of the French planters; while John Dickinson spoke of the British in the following slurring terms: "By a very singular disposition of affairs, the colonies of an *absolute monarchy* [France] are settled on a *republican principle;* while those of a kingdom in many respects *resembling a commonwealth* [England] are cantoned out among a *few lords* vested with despotic power over *myriads of vassals* and supported in the pomp of *Baggas* by *their* slavery."[4]

In short, foreign sugar and molasses could be had cheaper by from 25 to 40 per cent: it is not hard to see, therefore, why Northern colonial ship captains should take increasingly to buying their sugar at the foreign islands. They found it possible also to develop new markets here for their flour, provisions, lumber, work animals and fish, thus obtaining another source from which specie and bills of exchange could be derived. So great had this traffic become by the 1720's that the British planter interest took alarm and began to appeal to Parliament for succor: in 1733, Parliament yielded to pressure and passed the Molasses Act, which sought to outlaw the colonial-foreign island trade by placing prohibitive import duties on sugar, molasses and rum. But the act did not have the desired effect because it could not be adequately enforced: the British customs machinery in the colonies was weak and venal and the naval patrols that could be allocated to this duty were inadequate because of England's engagements in foreign wars from 1740 almost continuously for twenty years. Within these twenty years the illicit intercourse with the foreign West Indies took on such great proportions that it virtually became the foundation of Northern colonial merchant capitalism. By the late 1750's, when the traffic was at its height, at least 11,500 hogsheads of molasses reached Rhode Island annually from the foreign

---

[4] Italics in original.

islands, as against 2,500 from the British; in Massachusetts the ratio was 14,500 to 500. In Massachusetts alone there were some sixty-three distilleries in 1750 and perhaps half that number existed in Rhode Island: the manufacture of rum undoubtedly was the most important single industrial enterprise existing in New England in the second quarter of the eighteenth century. Rum was a magical as well as a heady distillation: its fluid stream reached far Guinea, distant Newfoundland, remote Indian trading posts: and it joined slaves, gold dust, the mackerel and cod, and peltries with the fortunes of the New England trading enterprisers.

Peter Faneuil, regular church attendant, kindly, charitably disposed bachelor was one of the greatest of these. He traded all over the world, paying English duties on his cargoes when he had to, avoiding them when he could. He was interested, of course, in rum and slaves. The distinguished historian of New England, Weeden, speaks in the following bitter terms of one of Faneuil's ships, the *Jolly Bachelor:* "Did Peter slap his fair round belly and chuckle when he named the snow *Jolly Bachelor?* — or was it the sad irony of fate that the craft deliberately destined to be packed with human pains and to echo with human groans should in its very name bear the fantastic image of the luxury-loving chief owner? If these be the sources of profit and property, where is the liberty of Faneuil Hall, where the charity of good Peter's alms?"

It is not to be wondered, therefore, that British planters kept up a constant clamor for the enforcement of the laws and the total stoppage of the foreign island trade; in this they were joined by the merchants and manufacturers whose fortunes were linked with theirs, and the bankers and rentiers who saw their great capital investment in the British islands threatened with destruction unless the British West Indians once more obtained a monopoly of the production of sugar and molasses. The Northern colonial merchant capitalists were the foes of British prosperity. The very reasonable exposition of the situation coming from Rhode Island's governor attracted no sympathy; apparently, it was to be the British West Indies or the Northern colonies, and the stake involved in the former, as far as England was concerned, was far, far greater.

Wrote Governor Stephen Hopkins to England:

By the best computation I have seen, the quantity of flour made in these colonies yearly is such, that after all the English inhabitants, as well of the continent as of the islands, are fully supplied, with as much as they can consume with the year, there remains a surplusage of at least one hundred thousand barrels. The quantity of beef and pork remaining after the English are in like manner supplied is very large. The fish, not fit for the European market, and the lumber produced in the Northern colonies, so much exceed the market found for them in the English West Indies, that a vast surplusage remains that cannot be used. . . . From the money and goods produced by the sale of the surplusages, with many others of less consequence, sold by one means or other to the Spaniards, French and Dutch in America, the merchants of those Northern colonies are principally enabled to make their remittances to the mother country for the British manufactures consumed in them. . . .

Supposing this intercourse of the colonies with the Spanish, French and Dutch entirely stopped, the persons concerned in producing the surplusages will of course change the manner of their industry, and improvement and, compelled by necessity, must set about making those things they cannot live without, and now rendered unable to purchase from their mother country.

When, during the Seven Years' War, the colonial "Smuggling Interest" extended the bounds of its activities and openly set about supplying the French enemy of the mother country with provisions, lumber, drygoods and the like, British sugar planters in Parliament, confronted by bankruptcy, found ready allies in outraged patriotic statesmen. Then it was that Pitt, deeply angered by knowledge of the open sale by colonial officials of commissions for flags of truce and the winking at the whole illegal practice by vice-admiralty courts, bitterly wrote to America that it was "an illegal and most pernicious trade . . . by which the enemy is, to the greatest reproach and detriment of government, supplied with provisions and other necessaries, whereby they are principally, if not alone, enabled to sustain and protract this long and expensive war." The process of repression began in 1760 with the stricter enforcement of the Acts of Trade and Navigation; from thence on, particularly after the last imperial rival, France, had been disposed of and the country at last was at peace, the screws came to be applied tighter and tighter. Soon, Northern merchant capitalists, aware that every avenue of continued activity was being blocked to them, moved into the colonial revolutionary host.

VII

It has been said that the mercantilist policy of English merchant capitalism demanded that the economic life of the American colonies be kept subservient to that of the mother country. From the very beginning — certainly, at any rate, from the turn of the eighteenth century when merchant capitalism was fully installed in the economy of the empire and in possession of its prerogative power — this was so: and a governmental apparatus was set up whose purpose it was consciously and constantly to maintain the imperial-colonial connection in this relationship. The real significance of all those imperial administrative agencies — the Privy Council, the Board of Trade, the Secretary of State in charge of Colonial Affairs, the Commissioners of Customs, the Treasury, the Admiralty and the royal governors — lay in the fact not that they created political or constitutional ties to unite colonies to the mother country but that they forged the fetters that bound the colonial merchant capitalism to that of England.

An examination of the activities of the imperial administrative agencies will plainly indicate that such an economic policy was consistently pursued: the period after 1763 merely marked its intensification as a result of the sharpening of the contradictions that appeared in mercantilism itself. The Board of Trade had been established in 1696, as O. M. Dickerson[5] points out, largely "to make the colonies commercially profitable to the mother country." And this it sought to do, over a period of more than three-quarters of a century, with a devotion and singleness of purpose that left small room for complaint. The commissioners, of course, made it their business to keep the Privy Council and Parliament informed as to the progress of the oversea possessions; but their powers were more than reportorial, for through four specific devices they were able to direct and supervise closely the economic development of the colonies. The Board of Trade was more or less in charge of preparing

[5] See his important and pioneer monograph, *American Colonial Government, 1695–1765* (Cleveland, 1912).

the colonial civil list, and it was also its function to supervise the activities of the colonial judiciary: by control over personnel its influence therefore was measurable. But more important were: first, its power to review colonial legislation and, if the purposes of provincial statutes ran counter to the welfare of the mother country, recommend their disallowance by the Privy Council; and second, its power to prepare specific instructions to the governors for their guidance in the exercise of the veto over colonial encroachments on the privileges and prerogatives of English citizens.

There were at least a dozen points at which the Board of Trade (representing English merchant capitalism) and the colonial legislatures (representing colonial merchant capitalism) constantly were in conflict, exactly because of the clash of economic interests. The outstanding of these were: colonial interference with the mother country's hold on foreign trade and shipping; attempts by the colonies to control the traffic in convicts and slaves; and colonial efforts to permit the payment of quit rents in paper money, to lower interest rates, to ease the judicial burdens imposed on debtors and to monopolize the Indian trade for colonials. Most important were the stern checks imposed by the Board of Trade on attempts by the colonial assemblies to encourage native manufacturing and to relieve the oppression of debts (because every section of colonial America, as we have seen, was in a debtor relationship toward England) through the increase of the money supply of the colonies.

In order to maintain the English control over trade and commerce, the Board of Trade recommended and obtained the disallowance by the Privy Council of legislation placing export duties on colonial raw materials needed by English enterprise; it was equally successful in outlawing acts whose purpose it was, through the grant of exemptions, to favor colonial shipowners in the carrying trade; and it ceaselessly moved against measures placing import duties on foreign wines and liquors and on English merchandise. Finally, when this last threatened to become a general practice, the Board issued blanket instructions to the governors ordering them to veto laws placing duties on European goods imported in English vessels (1724) and on the produce or manufactures of Great Britain (1732), and all those laws under which the natives of a province were given preferential treatment over those of Great Britain (1732).

The Privy Council repeatedly was called upon to disallow legislation laying high or prohibitive duties upon the importation of Negro slaves and interfering with the free transport of convicted felons overseas. The colonies for the most part were moving to protect themselves against the growth of undesirable elements in their population; although the motives of revenue and the protection of the quality of the slaves also were present. But the Board and the Privy Council were not unmindful of the great English slave-carrying trade that was bound to be affected by such legislation: its solicitude therefore was plain. Finally, in 1731, when the colonies persisted in their efforts to pass such bills, circular instructions were sent to the governors ordering them to veto legislation interfering with the free importation of Negroes and felons.

VIII

When colonies sought to foster local manufacturing enterprise, the Board of Trade could be expected to exercise an unceasing vigilance. Partly due to the abundance of raw materials and the constantly growing market but largely because of the accumulation of capital surpluses won in trade, colonial merchant capitalists always were pressing for the passage of laws to help the development of native industries. They obtained them: and colonial statute books, therefore, were filled with legislation that was, in effect, only modeled after those acts Parliament itself was passing: measures calling for the payment of bounties to private enterprisers and the extension of public credit to them, for exemptions from taxation, for easy access to raw materials, for the maintenance of standards of quality and for the encouragement of the location of new towns and of the settling of artisans in new and old urban communities.

Against such legislation the Board of Trade regularly moved; more than the colonial manufacturing of woolen goods, hats and wrought iron therefore was outlawed. Thus, in 1705, a Pennsylvania law for building up the shoemaking industry was disallowed on the ground that, as the Board said, "it cannot be expected that encouragement should be given by law to the making any manufactures made in England . . . , it being against the advantage of England." And in 1706, a New York law for developing the sailcloth industry was disallowed because, said the Board, it would be "more advantageous to England that all hemp and flax of the growth of the plantations should be imported hither, in order to manufacturing of it here." And in 1756, a Massachusetts law for encouraging the production of linen was disallowed on the general ground that "the passing of laws in the plantations for encouraging manufactures, which any ways interfere with the manufacture of this kingdom, has always been thought improper, and

has ever been discouraged." Nothing was too minute to escape the Board's attention in its zeal to protect England merchant capitalism. So, in 1706, 1707 and 1708, it went so far as to call for the rejection of laws passed in Virginia and Maryland providing for the establishment of new towns, on the grounds that such new communities must invariably lead to a desire to found manufacturing industries and that their existence would draw off persons from the countryside where they were engaged in the production of tobacco. To cap it all, the governors were closely instructed to veto all legislation designed to assist the development of such manufactures as might compete with those of England; this had its effect, so that E. B. Russell,[6] the outstanding authority upon the subject, has been led to conclude: "Largely as a result of the government's determined attitude in the matter, comparatively few laws for this purpose were enacted in the plantations."

The Board of Trade, always supported by Parliament, was equally vigilant in safeguarding the interests of English merchant capitalism in the financial sphere. It has been pointed out how the colonies, under the mercantilist system, were kept almost constantly in a debtor status within the imperial-colonial relations: and how their plight was accentuated by the insistence upon the payment of colonial unfavorable balances in specie. It has also been indicated how illegal activities — piracy, smuggling, trade with the foreign sugar islands — were compulsory precisely because of these unrelaxing pressures. The heavy burden of debts, therefore, the paucity of specie, and the

[6] See his monograph *The Review of American Colonial Legislation by the King in Council* (New York, 1915).

absence of easy credit facilities made all the colonies steadily preoccupy themselves with the money question: efforts to debase the currency, on the part of the colonies and, contrariwise, efforts to maintain it at a high value, on the part of England, were symptomatic of the disharmony that existed within the mercantilist framework. When, in 1764, all the devices at the service of the Board of Trade having failed, Parliament passed its act (the so-called Currency Act) outlawing the use of legal-tender paper money in all the colonies, it was apparent that the crisis had been reached: whether it meant universal breakdown for the colonial economic life or not, England was going to insist that debts be paid in pounds sterling in order to protect English merchant capitalism.

The colonies resorted to innumerable means to expand their available money supply. They employed commodity money, the assemblies fixing the value; but Parliament warned the colonists that they could not impair contracts by fixing rates for commodities contrary to those stipulated in agreements. They tried to mint their own money; but in 1684 colonial mints were forbidden. They sought to place embargoes on the exportation of coin; but beginning with 1697 the Privy Council regularly disallowed such laws. They tried, by statute, to raise the legal value of foreign coins in circulation, particularly the Spanish pieces of eight; such acts in Maryland and Virginia (and in Barbados and Jamaica) were disallowed, and when, as a result, the tobacco and sugar colonies were drained entirely of coin, in 1704 Parliament proceeded to fix a uniform value for pieces of eight in all the plantations and in 1708 prescribed prison sentences for those failing to observe the regulations.

Beginning as early as 1690, in Massachusetts, the colonies turned to the emission of paper money. This currency started out by being short-term bills of credit issued in anticipation of taxes (and therefore retirable at fixed dates after the taxes had been collected) and to be employed only for public purposes: the enactments specifically declared that the bills were not to be held as lawfully current money and could be submitted only in payment of public obligations. Within the first third of the eighteenth century, all of New England, as well as New York, New Jersey, the two Carolinas, Pennsylvania and Maryland had emitted such bills. It was an inevitable corollary that the bills of credit next be declared legal tender not only for public but for all private transactions: the intention was a sorely needed currency expansion, to be pursued by the road of a paper inflation. The steps by which the various colonies sought to attain this end may be briefly indicated: some tried to issue bills based not only on tax anticipations but on private land securities (utilizing the agency of public and private mortgage banks); some pushed the dates of collection of taxes on which the bills were based so far ahead that the issues virtually became permanent paper currency; some failed to provide adequate taxes from which the bills were to be redeemed; and some colonies openly embarked on a course of repudiation, merely reissuing bills when the dates set for cancellation had arrived. Also, steps were taken to compel the acceptance of these bills as legal tender by fixing penalties to be imposed on those individuals refusing to honor them in private transactions.

The establishment of so-called public banks, which really were agencies for the issuance of notes against the security of land mortgages, was particularly common. The first such provincial institution was set up in South Carolina and before 1750 every colony except Georgia had followed its example. Massachusetts went a step further when it permitted a group of private individuals to organize a "Land and Manufactures Bank" in 1740; this society, capitalized at £150,000, was to accept land as security for its stock and against this real estate it was to print notes to be used for lending purposes. Stockholders were to pay 3 per cent interest for the privilege of putting up their land as security, to be paid either in bills of the company or in non-perishable raw materials or rough manufactures (hence the use of the term "manufactures" in the title); also, every year 5 per cent of the principle of the subscription was to be amortized in the same way. Loans, too, could be paid off in bills or in the same commodities. The purpose here, obviously, was the expansion of credit through the utilization of non-perishable commodities as a base for currency issue; and within the single year of its operation the bank succeeded in lending out and therefore issuing notes to the extent of £40,000. But Parliament insisted upon regarding the bank as a dangerous speculative enterprise and descended on it at once; it extended to it the terms of the Bubble Act of 1720 and the bank was outlawed.

A notion of the mounting size of the paper currency in circulation may be gained from the experiences of Massachusetts. When this province emitted its first bills in 1690, it was ordered that the issues should not exceed £40,000; by 1750, however, some £4,630,000 in bills had been released, of which fully half still remained outstanding. Depreciation was inevitable. In Massachusetts, the value of sterling to paper money reached a maximum ratio of 11 to 1; in Connecti-

cut it was 8 to 1; in New Hampshire it got to 24 to 1 and by 1771 sterling had vanished altogether; in Rhode Island it was 26 to 1; in North Carolina it was 10 to 1; in South Carolina it was 7 to 1. Only in New York and Pennsylvania was there some effort made to check the downward career of the bills, the depreciation here never reaching more than 25 per cent.

It was the steadfast English policy to maintain a sound (that is to say, a contracted) currency in the colonies; and provincial acts were closely scrutinized from this point of view. Acts were disallowed and instructions issued, as affecting bills of credit, therefore, on the basis of the following general principles: that the amount of bills to be issued was to be limited to the minimum requirements necessary for the legitimate needs of the colonies; that there be created adequate provisions for refunding; that the term of issues be fixed and no reissues be permitted; and that the bills could not be made legal tender for the payment of private debts. Finally, when these methods seemed to be without avail, Parliament was resorted to. It has already been pointed out with what swiftness Parliament acted in the case of the Massachusetts land bank. A decade later, in 1751, an act was passed forbidding the New England colonies to make any further issues of legal tender bills of credit or bank notes; the only exceptions permitted were in the case of issues to cover current expenses or to finance war costs. And in 1764, by the Currency Act, the prohibition was extended to include all the colonies, even the exception in the case of military financing being rescinded; further, provision was to be made for the retirement of all outstanding bills. The currency immediately began to contract; and by 1774 there was not much more than £2,400,000 in the colonies available for exchange and the financing of the credit operations of colonial enterprise. John Dickinson was scarcely exaggerating the plight of colonial merchant capitalism when in 1765 he wrote:

Trade is decaying and all credit is expiring. Money is becoming so extremely scarce that reputable freeholders find it impossible to pay debts which are trifling in comparison to their estates. If creditors sue, and take out executions, the lands and personal estates, as the sale must be for ready money, are sold for a small part of what they were worth when the debts were contracted. The debtors are ruined. The creditors get back but part of their debt and that ruins them. Thus the consumers break the shopkeepers; they break the merchants; and the shock must be felt as far as London.

IX

This is the pattern of imperial-colonial relations which makes the events of 1763–1775 intelligible. Not human stupidity, not dreams of new splendor for the empire, not a growing dissimilarity of psychological attitudes, but economic breakdown in the mercantilist system: the inability of both English merchant capitalism and colonial merchant capitalism to operate within a contracting sphere in which clashes of interest were becoming sharper and sharper: such was the basic reason for the onset of crisis and the outbreak of revolutionary struggle. The mother country had bound the colonies to itself in an economic vassalage: opportunities for colonial enterprise were possible only in commercial agriculture (supported by land speculation) and in trade. But when the expanding commercial activities of Northern merchant capitalists came into conflict with the great capitalist interest of British West Indian

sugar and the related merchant and banking groups dependent upon it; when the Southern tobacco and rice planters, in their rôle of land speculators, collided with English land speculators and the mighty fur interest; and when colonial pressure to expand into manufacturing and to develop adequate credit facilities for its growing enterprises threatened the very existence of English merchant capitalism in all its ramifications: then repression, coercion, even the violence of economic extinction (as in the case of the Boston Port Bill) had to be resorted to. There could be no accommodation possible when English statesmen were compelled to choose between supporting English merchant capitalism and supporting colonial merchant capitalism.

As Professor Nettels has so justly insisted, American scholars for more than a generation have been led astray by George Louis Beer's erroneous interpretation of the motives that prompted Pitt in 1763 to demand Canada instead of the sugar islands Guadeloupe, Martinique and St. Lucia from vanquished France. Pitt had great visions of empire: and it was this dream and the imperial policies that stemmed from it that prepared the way for conflict between colonies and mother country. For a mighty western empire, based as yet on a wilderness, demanded the formulation of a wise program with regard to the Indian problem – hence the shutting off of the lands beyond the crest of the Alleghenies to further settlement and the checks placed on the exploitation of the Indians by colonial traders; it demanded a system of defence – hence the dispatching of a British army to the colonies and provisions for its quartering and maintenance; it demanded a revenue – hence all those methods resorted to by a hardpressed home government to develop new sources of financing. Thus the chain of circumstances was completed; it had to snap at its weakest link — the raising of funds through tax measures among a liberty-loving and individualistic colonial people which too long had been permitted to go its own way. So Mr. Beer, and after him virtually every American colonial scholar.

The events of 1763–1775 can have no meaning unless we understand that the character of English imperial policy was never changed: that Pitt and his successors at Whitehall were following exactly the same line that Cromwell had laid down more than a century before; that the purpose of the general program was to protect the English capitalist interests which now were being jeopardized as a result of the intensification of colonial capitalist competition; and that English statesmen yielded quickly when a fundamental principle was not at stake and only became more insistent when one was being threatened. If in the raising of a colonial revenue lay the heart of the difficulty, how are we to account for the quick repeal of the Stamp Tax and the Townshend Acts and the lowering of the molasses duty? And, on the other hand, how are we to account for the tightening of enforcement of the Acts of Trade and Navigation at a dozen and one different points, the passage of the Currency Act, the placing of iron on the enumerated list, English seizure of control of the wine trade, and the attempt to give the East India Company a monopoly over the colonial tea business? The struggle was not over high-sounding political and constitutional concepts: over the power of taxation and, in the final analysis, over natural rights: but over colonial manufacturing, wild lands and furs, sugar, wine, tea and currency, all of which meant, simply, the survival or collapse of English merchant capitalism within the imperial-colonial framework of the mercantilist system.

X

Even before Pitt gave up the French sugar islands in 1763 because of the insistence of the British sugar interest in Parliament, he had already moved to protect the same monopoly group through his orders to the navy to stamp out colonial smugglers operating in the illicit foreign West Indian trade. The colonial courts were directed to issue and recognize the doubtfully legal writs of assistance (general search warrants), as early as 1761. Two years later, the peace-time navy was converted into a patrol fleet with powers of search even on the high seas. In the same year, absentee officials in the customs service were ordered to their colonial posts. A vice-admiralty court was set up for all America in 1764 and the number of local admiralty courts (sitting without juries) was increased. In 1768 a new board of five customs commissioners to be resident in America was created. By statutes, by orders, by instructions, every conceivable weapon was employed to break up a traffic and therefore to weaken a group so dangerous to English capitalist interests. Spying was encouraged by offers to share with informers the sequestered cargoes; customs officials were protected from damage suits for unwarranted seizures when they were declared non-liable personally and when the burden of proof was placed on the owners of vessels and goods; the stricter registration and inspection of vessels were ordered; to protect informers and make possible the easier obtaining of verdicts, it was provided that suits for the seizure of cargoes might be tried directly in the vice-admiralty court and that revenue cases might be heard in the admiralty instead of the local courts; and to further free the courts from local pressure, the payment of the salaries of judges was to be made out of customs revenues.

The revenue acts of 1764 and later were used as a screen behind which the work of compressing within even narrower limits the economy of colonial merchant capitalism and of fastening tighter on it a dependent status was to go on. The Act of 1764 and the Stamp Act of 1765 called for the payment of duties and taxes in specie, thus further draining the colonies of currency and contracting the credit base. To divert colonial capital into raw materials, the first measure increased the bounties paid for the colonial production of hemp and flax, placed high duties on the colonial importation of foreign indigo, and removed the English import duties on colonial whale fins. To cripple the trade with the foreign West Indies a high duty was placed on refined sugar. The importation of foreign rum was forbidden altogether, and lumber was placed on the enumerated list. To give English manufacturers a firmer grip on their raw materials, hides and skins (needed for the boot-and-shoe industry), pig and bar iron (needed in the wrought iron industry), and potash and pearl ashes (used for bleaching cloth and hence needed in the woolen industry), were placed on the enumerated list. To maintain the English monopoly of the colonial finished-goods market in 1764 the entrance into the colonies of certain kinds of French and Oriental drygoods was taxed for the first time; in 1765, the importation of foreign silk stockings, gloves and mitts was altogether forbidden; also the drawbacks of duties paid on foreign goods landed in England and re-exported to the colonies were rescinded. To extend the market of English merchants in Europe, in 1766 Parliament ordered that all remaining non-enumerated articles (largely flour, provisions and fish) bound for European ports north of Cape Finisterre be landed first in England. And to weaken further colonial commercial activity, in 1764 high duties were placed on wines from the wine islands and wine, fruits and oil from Spain and Portugal brought directly to America (in American ships, as a rule), while such articles brought over from England were to pay only nominal duties.

As has been said, the revenue features of these acts were quickly abandoned; the Stamp Act was repealed; and in 1770, three years after their passage, the Townshend duties on paper, paint and glass were lifted. Only the slight tax on tea remained and even this was lightened in 1773 when the new Tea Act provided for a full drawback of English import duties on British tea shipped to the American colonies.

But it was exactly this new Tea Act which clearly revealed the intention of London: that not only was the economic vassalage of the American colonies to be continued but the interest of colonial enterprisers was to be subordinated to every British capitalist group that could gain the ear of Parliament. For, to save the East India Company from collapse, that powerful financial organization was to be permitted to ship in its own vessels and dispose of, through its own merchandising agencies, a surplus stock of 17,000,000 pounds of tea in America: and, in this way, drive out of business those Americans who carried, imported and sold into retail channels British tea (and indeed, foreign tea, for the British tea could be sold cheaper even than the smuggled Holland article). The merchants all over America were not slow to read the correct significance of this measure. Their spokesmen sounded the alarm. As Arthur M. Schlesinger[7] has put it, pamphleteers set out to show "that the present project of the East India Company was the entering wedge for larger and more ambitious undertakings calculated to undermine the colonial mercantile world. Their opinion was based on the fact that, in addition to the article of tea, the East India Company imported into England vast quantities of silks, calicos and other fabrics, spices, drugs and chinaware, all commodities of staple demand; and on their fear that the success of the present venture would result in an extension of the same principle to the sale of the other articles." The result would be, as a Philadelphia pamphleteer signing himself "A Mechanic" warned:

They will send their own factors and creatures, establish houses among us, ship us all other East India goods; and in order to full freight their ships, take in other kinds of goods at under freight, or (more probably) ship them on their own accounts to their own factors, and undersell our merchants, till they monopolize the whole trade. Thus our merchants are ruined, ship building ceases. They will then sell goods at any exorbitant price. Our artificers will be unemployed, and every tradesman will groan under dire oppression.

By 1773, therefore, it was plain that America was to be sacrificed: colonial merchant capitalists were compelled to strike back through the destruction of the tea and the writing and enforcement of the Continental Association.

XI

The blows aimed at colonial merchant capitalism through the strengthening of

[7] See his distinguished monograph, *The Colonial Merchants and the American Revolution, 1763–1776* (New York, 1917).

the Acts of Trade and Navigation, the promulgation of the Proclamation Line of 1763 and the passage of the Currency Act of 1764 precipitated the crisis in the imperial-colonial relations: and merchant capitalists (whether land speculators or traders) were soon converted from contented and loyal subjects into rebellious enemies of the crown. But, to be successful, the revolutionary host had to be swelled from the ranks of the lower middle-class small farmers and traders and the working-class artisans, mechanics, seamen, fishermen and lumbermen. This was not difficult: for the material well-being of the lower classes was tied to the successful enterprising of the upper, and contraction of economic opportunity in the higher sphere was bound to bring want and suffering in the lower.

The colonies had enjoyed a period of unprecedented prosperity during the Seven Years' War: the expanding market in the West Indies, the great expenditures of the British quartermasters, the illegal and contraband trade with the enemy forces, all had furnished steady employment for workers and lucrative outlets for the produce of small farmers. But with the end of the war and the passage of the restrictive legislation of 1763 and after, depression had set in. With stringency and bankruptcy everywhere confronting merchant capitalists, it was inevitable that mechanics, artisans, seamen and lumbermen should be thrown out of employment, small tradesmen should be compelled to close the doors of their shops, and that small farmers should be confronted with an expanded acreage, a diminished market and heavy fixed charges made even more onerous as a result of currency contraction. Into the bargain, escape into the frontier zones — always the last refuge of the dispossessed — was shut off. Openly abetted by merchants and land speculators, the lower classes moved into the revolutionary host.

It would be a mistake to assume, however, that the working class and lower middle-class groups surrendered up their identities completely and operated only at the behest and with the encouragement of the merchant capitalists. Under the direction of their own leaders in the Sons of Liberty and the Committees of Correspondence, they were able to articulate their own class demands: the result was, the period of revolutionary crisis saw the development of a radical program which merchants and planters regarded with misgivings and dread but with which they dared not interfere lest, in alienating the underprivileged farmers, tradesmen and workers, they lose that mass support upon which their own destiny so completely was dependent. The lower classes began to look upon the revolution as the instrument for attaining their freedom: from the civil disability of almost universal disfranchisement, from the inequalities of entail and primogeniture, from oppression at the hands of engrossing landlords and from the threatened dominance and exactions of an oversea ecclesiastical authority.

For these and similar class reasons, the lower middle classes and the workers of colonial America joined with the merchants and planters in demonstrations against the imperial program: and when peaceful agitation and pressure proved unavailing, they were ready to take up arms when England resorted to coercion and violence. In 1774 and 1775, through the agencies of the Coercive Acts and the Restraining Acts, England, by striking at the economic life of the colonies directly, virtually opened hostilities. The colonists replied with two declarations of freedom. The first, naturally representing the dominant interest of merchant capitalism, was embodied in a series of resolutions passed by the Second Continental Congress, 6 April, 1776; these nullified the Acts of Trade and Navigation and put an end to the colonial slave trade: and with this single blow colonial merchant capitalism smashed the hampering fetters of the imperial-colonial relations. The second, adopted by the Congress, 4 July, 1776, was the Declaration of Independence: written by the radicals, this was a political manifesto which called upon the masses to defend the revolution. The first American Revolution then moved fully into the stage of armed resistance.

Charles M. Andrews:

A NOTE ON THE ECONOMIC INTERPRETATION OF THE AMERICAN REVOLUTION

WRITERS of the economic deter-minist school, who of late years have been reviving a faith in the eco-nomic interpretation of history and seek-ing a place in the historical sunshine, believe that the Revolution was either an attempt of "the American merchant and planter-capitalism" to obtain "release from the fetters of the English Mercan-tile System" (Hacker, *The First Ameri-can Revolution* and *A Graphic History*) or a movement "to free [America] from the colonial ban upon her industries" (Beard, *A History of the Business Man*).

These and other similar theses can be maintained only by a system of clever, ingenious, and seemingly plausible but really superficial manipulations of fact and logic in the interest of a precon-ceived theory; by generalizations based on the grouping of occasional and widely scattered data; and by dependence on the statements of secondary authorities — statements frequently unfortified by proof and sometimes demonstrably un-true. Even Dr. Lipson, a writer not averse to an economic interpretation of history and one whose opinions the economic determinists are inclined to respect, is unable to accept these ex-planations and sums up the situation as follows.

The extent to which economic factors were responsible for the American Revolution can-not easily be measured. At first sight it is natural to attribute the disruption of Eng-land's first empire to a policy avowedly de-signed to make the oversea settlements "duly subservient and useful." Yet contemporary English opinion held that the colonies "felt the benefit more than the burden" of the Acts of Trade, and the view appears on the whole well-founded. Irksome as their disabilities may seem on paper, the working of the sys-tem was not unduly onerous in practice. It was modified by concessions such as those which enabled the colonies to carry on trade direct with southern Europe in certain "enu-merated commodities," or it was evaded with the open connivance of the American author-ities. This lax administration of the system helped to bring the authority and prestige of the mother country into disrepute; and habit-ual disregard for the laws of the parent state fostered a spirit of independence, which made any attempt at enforcement of the laws appear a gross act of tyranny. The efforts to suppress smuggling and administer the Acts of Trade with greater rigour, by substituting vice-admiralty courts for juries and employ-ing the navy, were the more deeply resented because the colonies had grown accustomed to the latitude which alone made the Acts tolerable. Against their disabilities, real or nominal, must be set the reciprocal advan-tages which the colonies enjoyed in the shape of the protection, the credit and the market of the mother country. The old colonial system, as the ruthless destruction of tobacco-growing in England demonstrated, was far from one-sided. Nor were even their disabilities unattended by compensating features. Behind the shelter of the Navigation Laws which protected her from alien competition, New England built up an important shipbuilding industry. These considerations may fairly lead us to conclude that, though individuals chafed against the restraints laid upon them, the colonies would not have cut themselves adrift from the mother country on the ground of economic grievances alone: and this conclusion is fortified by the absence, in the Declaration of Independence, of all reference to the Acts of Trade beyond an allusion of doubtful significance (*Economic History of England*, 2d ed., III, 194–196).

This is not the place to discuss the conclusions reached, but something may be said, very briefly. In the first place, there never was a hard and fast "Mercantile System" and British governmental policy, which in the long run was responsible for the Revolution, was never identical with the mercantilist programme, even before 1763 when mercantilism was in the ascendant. The government had to consider the needs of the state and the exchequer, the constitutional rights of the prerogative, and the legislative authority of parliament as well as the wishes and prosperity of the merchant-capitalists. After 1763, British colonial policy, though still favoring the merchants, was in many of its most important parts distinctly at odds with them. The Proclamation of 1763, the Stamp Act, the Declaratory Act, the Quebec Act of 1774, and the Carleton commission and instructions of 1775, were none of them mercantilist in their objectives. With equal truth may it be said that the Sugar Act, the trade acts of 1764–1766, and the Townshend Acts were designed much more in the interest

of the revenue which the exchequer greatly needed than of the business prosperity of the capitalists. In 1766, the Board of Trade itself, often construed as under the thumb of the mercantilists, in defining British policy, added to "The Commerce and Manufactures of this Country" two other ends to be sought, "Your Majestys Royal Prerogative and the Authority of the British Legislature." At the same time the board made it abundantly clear that its own members, as well as the executive departments of government, were interpreting colonial policy, not in terms of the merchants' profits, but of the financial solvency of the British Exchequer, for the war debt after 1763 amounted to £140,000,000. The British government had other interests at stake than those of the merchants and always found it difficult to satisfy the merchants as much as the merchants wished to be satisfied, a situation of which the latter frequently complained. It is sheer assumption to assert that in England at this time the acts of the executive and the legislation of parliament were necessarily determined by business pressure, for the one thing the mercantilists did not want was parliamentary taxation of the colonies.

In the second place, the colonists must have known where the shoe pinched most painfully. Those of New England did protest against the measures of the years 1764–1766 and the Townshend Acts of 1767 and nearly all the colonists tried without success to neutralize them by non-consumption and non-importation devices, but in these ventures they were not preparing for revolution nor were they doing anything more than attempting to obtain a redress of trade grievances and to bring the British parliament to terms. The non-importation movement was at first a protest against commercial restraints and financial impositions and was initiated chiefly by the merchants. But as time went on it passed out of the control of the merchants into the hands of those to whom trade was a secondary consideration and who, as individualists and political agitators, were concerned for what they called "human rights and liberties." These men gave prominence, not to trade grievances which, had no other grievances intervened, would probably have been eventually redressed, but to a constitutional claim that parliament would not recognize as a claim deserving of any consideration. Behind this claim, which at bottom represented simply the determination of each of the colonies to manage its own affairs, lay a great variety of local grievances — financial, territorial, governmental, and religious — grievances that actuated each colony to uphold the larger claim, as one which all could support. It is untrue to fact to say that there was any one grievance common to all, and that grievance solely commercial or industrial.

The constitutional issue appears as early as 1765 and, as the commercial and financial complaints dwindled in importance with the failure of the non-importation movement, it became the leading issue after 1770. From this time forward, though economic grievances still occasionally appear and the retention of the tea tax made trouble, the constitutional claim dominates the scene and freedom from outside control, in many ways at that time much more a grievance than were matters that concerned trade and manufacturing, became the real objective. In very few, if any, of the resolutions of towns and local assemblies, the memorials and other official papers of the First Continental Congress, and the Declaration of Independence (which contains only one item out of twenty-seven constituting an economic grievance) is there anything suggesting a "release from the fetters of the English Mercantile System" or a desire to be freed from any ban on colonial industries. On the contrary the Declaration and Resolves of the First Continental Congress expressly state, "we cheerfully consent to the operation of such acts of the British parliament, as are bona fide restrained to the regulation of our external commerce, for the purpose of securing the commercial advantages of the whole Empire to the mother country, and the commercial benefits of its respective members." Over and over again the protestants in America ask for nothing more than to return to the "state of harmony and unity" that prevailed before 1763 — a state which they considered "beneficial to the whole empire and as ardently desired by all America." They wanted so to return despite the fact that before 1763 the aims of the British authorities were much more nearly identified with the wishes of the mercantilists than they were afterward, though even during this earlier period the government hedged a good deal in meeting mercantilist demands. It is a gross historical blunder to start with the premises that British colonial policy and mercantilism were at any time convertible terms or that the colonists were ever seriously hampered by the restrictions placed upon their desire to manufacture.

One may not doubt that behind the effort to obtain self-government and freedom from the restraints of British control there lay factors that were commercial, financial, legal, social, and industrial. But no one of these by itself would have brought on the Revolution. It is too great a simplification of history to regard the events of the past as nothing but a struggle of classes, a clash of economic interests, for such an oversimplification of the problem leads inevitably to an oversimplified solution. No amount of study of the social side of colonial life — much vaunted today as if it were something new — will explain the events of 1775 and 1776. It is never very difficult, by methods of grouping and omission, to phrase things in such a way as to lead to misrepresentation.` To emphasize the economic aspects to the exclusion of all else is to interpret human affairs in terms of material things only, to say nothing of the spiritual power necessary to use these material resources for human welfare, to ignore the influence of sentiment and morality, and to underrate the rich and varied stuff of human nature, the distractions of statesmen, and the waywardness and uncertainty of events.\The historian, if he is to keep both his levels and his proportions true, cannot fail to stress, first of all, the institutional and structural aspects of colonial life, which, despite certain present-day opinions to the contrary, are fundamental to any right understanding of the colonial past. At the same time if he is honest to himself and his evidence he cannot neglect the imponderable forces (always most difficult to identify and trace), as well as the driving influence of emotional and mass psychology. These factors are essential, however much those who can see in society, present and past, only things that are "real" and "practical" — business success and class warfare — and consider irrelevant whatever cannot be pinned down as a social or economic activity. No one should deal with the past whose ambition it is to find a single cause for all that has happened or who is unwilling to admit the existence of many causes acting simultaneously. Mr. J. A. Spender, sympathetic liberal and newspaper editor, can say, "There is as little probability of discovering one key to the problems of human society as there is of finding one remedy for the ills of the human body," and Mr. J. M. Keynes, the eminent economist, can add even more emphatically, "The view that the economic ideal is the sole respectable purpose of the community as a whole is the most dreadful heresy which has ever gained the ear of a civilized people."

Modern industrialism would seem to be responsible for these latter-day attempts to interpret the past in the light of the present and to apply the Marxian doctrine that social progress is the outcome of class conflict and of nothing else.

John C. Miller: THE ECONOMIC BACKGROUND
OF THE AMERICAN REVOLUTION

THE imposition of the mercantilist system exacted heavy sacrifices from the American colonies during the seventeenth century. Instead of the freedom of trade with the world which they had largely enjoyed prior to 1651, they were now confined for the most part to the markets of the mother country and other parts of the empire; and the colonial consumer was delivered over to the English merchant and manufacturer. From a free-trade area, the British Empire was transformed into a highly protected market closed to foreign competition. The losses in liberty and material prosperity attendant upon this economic reorganization of the empire were borne chiefly by the colonists; from the beginning, whether mercantilism appeared beneficent or oppressive depended largely from what side of the Atlantic it was viewed.

But as the mercantilists frequently pointed out, Americans were compensated for the restrictions imposed by the mother country upon their trade and commerce. Mercantilists did not advocate the exploitation by the mother country of the colonies: their ideal was rather an empire in which every part contributed to the best of its ability toward the goal of self-sufficiency; and they insisted that the good of the whole be made the guiding principle of the mother country's colonial policy. Accordingly, in exchange for the monopoly enjoyed by the mother country in the colonies, a virtual monopoly of the English market was given the

producers of certain colonial commodities. All foreign tobacco, for example, was excluded from England (although this restriction was later modified to permit the importation of some Portuguese and Spanish tobacco) and Englishmen were forbidden to plant tobacco in England — a law which was consistently violated until at the end of the seventeenth century the price of tobacco became so low that it was no longer profitable to grow it there. Moreover, tariff protection was given by the mother country to sugar, cotton, and indigo grown in the British colonies — thus placing a burden on the English consumer who, in an open market, undoubtedly could have bought cheaper. At the same time, bounties were given upon the production of naval stores, pitch, silk, and wine in the colonies — in the hope that the empire would become self-sufficient in these commodities and that Americans, if encouraged to produce raw materials, would be diverted from manufacturing for themselves.[1]

Yet despite the benefits of mercantilism, Americans surrendered their economic liberties grudgingly. They lamented that the Dutch traders who in the seventeenth century sold goods at one-third the price charged by English merchants came among them no longer

[1] *The Trade and Navigation of Great Britain Considered*, London, 1730, 79–80. *The Importance of the British Dominion in India Compared with that in America*, London, 1770, 13–14. Philip W. Buck, *The Politics of Mercantilism*, New York, 1942, 15.

From *Origins of the American Revolution* by John C. Miller, copyright 1943 by John C. Miller. Reprinted by permission of Little, Brown and Company.

and that in their stead appeared English-men who, as the governor of Virginia said, would "faine bring us to the same poverty, wherein the Dutch found and relieved us." Bacon's Rebellion was caused in part by the depression that struck Virginia in the wake of the Acts of Trade. The Massachusetts General Court declared in the seventeenth century that it would not obey the Navigation Acts because the people of Massachusetts were not represented in the English Parliament and because "the lawes of England are bounded within the fower seas, and do not reach America" — a more sweeping assertion of colonial rights than was made by Americans until 1776.

As Great Britain became increasingly industrialized during the eighteenth century, the chorus of complaint in the colonies against high-priced British goods subsided, although the Southern planters remained unreconciled to British monopoly. In general, the price of British manufactures declined and the quality improved to such a degree that it is doubtful if the colonists could have bought cheaper from their old friends the Dutch. This was not true, however, of India goods, of which large quantities were purchased by Americans, a substantial part being smuggled from Holland. But even so there was considerable foundation for the claim made by Englishmen in the eighteenth century that the Acts of Trade could not justly be regarded as a hardship by Americans inasmuch as they procured cheaper and better goods in England than could have been bought in France or Holland. Later, after the United States had achieved its independence, Lord Sheffield was to elaborate this argument into the theory — and win the British government to his view — that the

young republic was so inextricably bound to English economy that it could not break its bonds regardless of how inconsiderately it was treated by Great Britain.

New England did not readily fit into the mercantilists' scheme of a rightly ordered empire. Instead of busying themselves at home producing necessities for the mother country and exchanging them for English manufactures, the Puritans took to the sea with such vigor that it was said their commerce smelled as strongly of fish as their theology did of brimstone. Except for timber and masts, New England lacked valuable staples required by the mother country. And so New Englanders derived little advantage, in contrast to the Southern colonists, from English bounties: "A Cargo of any of them [bountied commodities] will be returned to us in a few Trunks of Fripperies," they said, "and we should be Bankrupt to Great Britain every Ten Years."[2]

The Puritans found that their salvation lay in manufacturing on their own and in pursuing that "coy mistress, trade" over a large part of the world in order to scrape together enough cash to pay for the goods they imported from Great Britain. During the colonial period, the exports of the Northern colonies to Great Britain were far less than their imports from her; but the merchants prospered despite this adverse balance of trade. By engaging in the slave trade, making rum, exploiting the fisheries, manufacturing for the Middle and Southern colonies as well as for their own use, and acting as middlemen between land-bound colonists and English businessmen, they found profitable outlet for their energy and capital. The freightage, commissions,

[2] *Providence Gazette and Country Journal,* February 9, 1765.

and charges for services and credits paid by the colonial consumer helped build the American seaports and laid the foundations for many of the early American fortunes. Herein the colonial merchants came into collision with the British merchants, who, by virtue of their vast financial resources, enjoyed a considerable advantage over their American rivals. But the colonists were by no means outclassed: ships could be built cheaper in New England than elsewhere in the British Empire; New Englanders possessed a canniness in trade that staggered even the Scotch; and they were masters of the art of slipping a cargo of contraband past the inefficient and undermanned colonial customhouse.

Under these circumstances, the American merchants found little quarrel with the Laws of Trade as they were actually enforced; they grew up under the system and — except for restrictions upon their trade with the foreign West Indies — were not unduly hampered by British commercial laws. The British Empire, they learned, was, in the main, big enough to hold both themselves and the British merchants, and so long as the mother country did not begrudge them a profit or too strictly enforce its laws they were in general well content. Given the lax enforcement of the Acts of Trade — by which the door was left ajar for highly profitable smuggling — and the advantages of carrying on business within the British Empire — one of the greatest trading areas in the world — it is not probable that the Navigation Acts alone would have produced a revolutionary spirit among American businessmen. On the contrary, the conviction was strongly established among many colonists that their economic well-being depended upon remaining within the empire and

enjoying the benefits of its highly protected markets.[3]

In the Middle colonies, where a far more even balance prevailed between agriculture and commerce than in New England, the Acts of Trade inflicted little appreciable hardship. These provinces exported large quantities of cereals and lumber to the European continent and the West Indies. It is important to observe in this connection that their trade with the West Indies, like that of the New England colonies, was not restricted to the British West Indies; the most profitable branch of their commerce was with the French, Dutch, and Spanish islands. Although this trade was not prohibited by the Navigation Acts, it ran counter to every principle of mercantilism and in 1733 was virtually prohibited by an act of Parliament which, as will be seen, proved unenforceable. In studying the origins of the American Revolution, it ought to be borne in mind that the prosperity of New England and the Middle colonies depended in a large measure upon a trade which had been built up outside the walls which mercantilists sought to erect around the empire.

Neither New England nor the Middle colonies were as intimately tied to the British market as were the staple colonies of the North American continent and the West Indies. Whereas the Northern colonies failed to produce vital raw materials required by the mother country and so fell short of the mercantilists' ideal, the Southern colonies fulfilled their highest expectations. These provinces constituted a rich agricultural area which supplied the mother country with such valuable

[3] For an opposing view see L. M. Hacker, "The First American Revolution," *Columbia University Quarterly*, September 1935, XXVII. [Reproduced on page 1. Ed.]

products as tobacco, naval stores, rice, indigo, cotton, and sugar — the chief staples of commerce — and received in exchange British-manufactured goods. These commodities were enumerated and the planters themselves had little opportunity to supplement their incomes by smuggling. Moreover, they were excellent customers of British merchants and manufacturers. While it is true that all the American colonies depended largely upon imports of manufactured articles from Great Britain to maintain a European living standard in the New World, the Southern staple colonies were so lacking in local industries that they were compelled to look to the mother country for virtually all their manufactured goods.

Mercantilists rejoiced in the Southern staple colonies as the jewels of the empire; but many planters found that the shoe of mercantilism pinched acutely. The tightness of the squeeze differed considerably, however, among the various kinds of planters. Although they were all more or less at the mercy of the British merchants and manufacturers who sold them goods and advanced them credit, some planters had secured preferential treatment from the mother country. In 1730, for example, the British government partially met the demands of the Carolina rice growers by permitting them to export rice — which had been enumerated by the British government in 1704 — to southern Europe, although they were still forbidden to import manufactures except through Great Britain. In 1739, the sugar planters of the West Indies were likewise given the privilege of exporting sugar directly to Europe although they produced barely enough to supply the needs of the British Empire alone. This concession was won largely because of the presence in the British Parliament of a powerful bloc of absentee West India planters aided by a lobby of West India merchants.[4] As a result, during the eighteenth century, the sugar colonies were in little danger of finding their interests sacrificed to those of the mother country or of the Northern colonies; on the contrary, the Northern colonists and the British consumer were in dire danger of being made the victims of West Indian cupidity.

No such advantages were enjoyed by the tobacco growers of Virginia and Maryland. Certainly as regards tobacco, Great Britain was not in any sense "the natural entrepôt for the American trade with the continent" which the Laws of Trade sought to make it — rather, it was a bottleneck through which the British government attempted to force colonial trade. Of the 96,000 hogsheads of tobacco sent by Maryland and Virginia to England each year, 82,000 were re-exported to the continent, competing there with Spanish tobacco; and this re-exported tobacco paid double freight, insurance, commissions, and handling charges. Daniel Dulany of Maryland estimated that the Southern tobacco growers would have received £3 more for every hogshead they sent abroad had they been permitted to ship direct to the continent instead of through England.[5] In addition, the British government insisted upon its pound of flesh from the planters. A heavy duty was imposed upon all tobacco imported into Great Britain; and from this source the government drew a revenue of almost £400,000 a year. The planters complained that this duty was

[4] F. W. Pitman, *The Development of the British West Indies,* New Haven, 1917, 182–188.

[5] Daniel Dulany, *Considerations on the Propriety of Imposing Taxes on the British Colonies,* London, 1766, 73–76. Adam Smith, *The Wealth of Nations,* New York, 1937, 568–569.

levied upon them rather than upon the British consumer and that they were thereby more heavily taxed than even the British squires.[6]

The reason why the planters, more than other Americans, found their lot galling under British mercantilism was partly owing to their practice of pledging future crops in exchange for credits advanced them by British businessmen. In order to protect themselves against loss, the British merchants charged the planters high prices and high interest rates. Of the £4,000,000 owing British merchants by Americans in 1760, over half had been incurred by Southern planters. It is not surprising, therefore, that from the point of view of the tobacco growers, the Acts of Trade seemed designed chiefly for the better exploitation of American producers. The American colonies were the West of the British Empire and the Southern gentry, despite their great landed estates, slaves, and aristocratic manners, maintained an attitude toward British merchants not far removed from that of a Dakota dirt farmer toward a Wall Street banker. They were resentful toward their creditors, whom they blamed bitterly for having loaned them money. Thomas Jefferson believed that the British merchants conspired to get planters in debt by at first paying good prices and offering easy credit; then, when the planter was securely in their toils, cutting prices until he was inextricably in debt. Thus, said Jefferson, did Virginia planters become "a species of property annexed to certain mercantile houses in London."[7] Washington complained that British merchants had beaten down the price of tobacco until its cultivation was no longer profitable, and turned to wheat to free himself from their stranglehold. The Southern growers also grumbled that British middlemen devoured the lion's share of the profits, leaving only a few well-picked bones for the hapless producers. They declared that "they send their produce home, which is sold by the merchants at their own price, and aded to this Considerable Charges, there was but little Comeing to the poor planter, and Even that litle was sent out to him in some necessary furniture which cost him as Dear in proportion as his tobacco was sold Cheap. thus the Inhabitants of america were allways from hand to mouth."[8] To the planters, almost every class in England seemed to be thrusting its hand into their pockets: "the Factors, the Carriers, the Shopkeepers, the Merchants, the Brokers, the Porters, the Watermen, the Mariners, and others," all fattened upon them. They declared that they were paying from 25 to 40 per cent more for manufactured goods than if they had enjoyed free trade with Europe: and Daniel Dulany calculated that "the Artificial Value of a Bale of English Cloth arising from Taxes, Monopolies and ill-judged Laws" was over 50 per cent of its original worth.[9]

Besides fleecing the planters by these methods, the merchants were accused by Marylanders and Virginians of abusing their privilege of monopolizing colonial trade by making the colonies a dumping ground for shopworn, unsalable merchandise; cheating on weights and meas-

---

6 *The True Interest of Great Britain, with respect to her American Colonies Stated and Impartially Considered*, London, 1766, 25, 42.

7 *The Writings of Thomas Jefferson*, edited by Paul Leicester Ford, New York, 1894, IV, 155.

8 *American Historical Review*, October 1921, XXVII, 74.

9 Dulany, 35, 73–76. *The American Gazette*, London, 1768–1769, 41. *Letters and Papers relating chiefly to the Provincial History of Pennsylvania*, Philadelphia, 1855, 213–214.

ures; and, what perhaps was most unforgivable of all to many Southerners, sending them goods which were not "genteel, well manufactured, and fashionable."[10]

No doubt the planters were less than just to their English creditors: there was no conspiracy to depress prices — in fact, the competition furnished by the Scotch merchants who were attempting to break into the tobacco trade tended to raise the prices of tobacco — and no convincing evidence was ever presented that the British merchants were cheating on weights. Nevertheless, the fact that the Southern planters believed themselves the victims of price-rigging and scale-juggling is significant in accounting for the hostility which they displayed toward the British government after 1765. The planters' debts, observed the governor of Virginia, made them "uneasy, peevish and ready to murmur at every Occurrence"; and Jonathan Boucher, a Church of England clergyman, concluded that the Southern gentry, despite their breeding and expensive tastes, were like conspirators and revolutionaries the world over: they were deeply in debt and eager to be free from their creditors.[11]

The low price of tobacco of which the planters complained was owing to circumstances over which the British merchants had no control. Tobacco consumption in England was leveling off after a long rise: it was said "multitudes have left off taking it" and that it had almost been cast out of "polite company."[12] The result was that tobacco prices fell but the planters refused to adjust their scale of living to new conditions: they continued to order luxuries from British merchants as usual and thus sank even more deeply into debt. Their contempt for trade likewise proved injurious to their interests. Disdaining commerce as unworthy of a gentleman, the planters were obliged to deal through resident Scottish and English representatives of the great British mercantile houses. These factors or merchants, particularly the Scotch, were regarded as an alien breed — money-grabbers and cheats who lived by defrauding the planters. Colonel Chiswell of Virginia called Robert Routledge, a merchant of Prince Edward County, a "fugitive rebel, a villain who came to Virginia to cheat and defraud men of their property, and a Presbyterian fellow." Whereupon the Colonel ran Routledge through with his sword, declaring as he applied the *coup de grâce,* "He deserves his fate, damn him; I aimed at his heart, and I have hit it." After which, "he called for a bowl of toddy, and drank it very freely."[13] Virginians complained that the Scotch merchants trading in America had raised Glasgow "from being a poor, small, petty Port, to one of the richest Towns and trading Ports in his Majesty's Dominions, and all by Fawning, Flattery, and outwitting the indolent and thoughtless Planters." It is significant that of the Tory property confiscated by Virginians during the Revolutionary War, one third

[10] *Proceedings and Debates of the British Parliament respecting North America,* edited by L. F. Stock, Washington, 1937, IV, 221. Essex Institute, *Historical Collections,* January 1927, LXIII, 28. *Principles and Acts of the Revolution,* edited by H. Niles, Boston, 1817, 67, note.

[11] *Governor Fauquier to the Earl of Halifax,* June 14, 1765, P.R.O., C.O., Class 5, 1345. Jonathan Boucher, *A View of the Causes and Consequences of the American Revolution,* London, 1797, xliii (preface).

[12] Dulany, 34. It is also clear that "soil exhaustion and the mounting burden of fixed charges and debt" contributed to the plight of colonial tobacco growers. A thorough discussion of this subject may be found in Curtis P. Nettels, *The Roots of American Civilization,* New York, 1938, 416–424.

[13] *Virginia Gazette* (Purdie and Dixon), July 18, 1766.

belonged to the hated Scotch merchants of Norfolk.[14]

The repeated intervention by the British government on behalf of the English and Scottish merchants certainly gave the planters no cause to love British imperialism. It was the home government which thwarted their attempts to pass laws making lands and Negroes freehold and therefore not liable to seizure as satisfaction for debts due British merchants. Again, it was the British government that disallowed their stay laws, moratoriums, and laws prohibiting the importation of slaves — thus preferring, as the colonists saw it, "the immediate advantage of a few African corsairs, to the lasting interests of the American states, and to the rights of human nature."[15]

It became increasingly clear to Americans during the eighteenth century that the British Empire was not, as the mercantilists envisaged, a government of Kings, Lords, and Commons in which the welfare of the whole empire was the chief concern of imperial legislation, but a government of British merchants and manufacturers who pursued their own interests even at the expense of the colonists. The prohibition of paper money as legal tender in the colonies forcibly brought home this conviction to many Americans. Undoubtedly, the colonists had abused their privilege of issuing paper money and the British merchants

had been the principal sufferers thereby. With considerable justification, the merchants complained that they found "more security, and better, & more speedy Justice in the most distant Provinces of the Ottoman Dominions from their Bashaws, than they do in some of the American Colonies, tho' under the Dominion of their own Prince." It became a proverb among the merchants that "if a Man goes over never so honest to the Plantations, yet the very Air there does change him in a short time."[16] In particular, it seemed to dispose him to pay his English creditors in depreciated paper money. Only the vigilance of the colonial governors and the Privy Council in disallowing colonial laws of this nature saved the merchants from ruin. Parliament was obliged to intervene repeatedly in their behalf: in particular, the act of the reign of George II which made lands and Negroes in the colonies subject to the payment of English debts was hailed as "the grand Palladium of Colony credit, and the English merchants' grand security." Nevertheless, the merchants insisted upon more drastic measures to prevent the colonists from wriggling out of their debts. They clamored above all for the prohibition of the colonial paper money with which they had repeatedly burned their fingers. The colonial creditor class joined in the chorus and in 1751 Parliament responded by passing an act which declared paper money illegal in New England; and in 1764 the issuance of paper money as legal tender was forbidden in all the colonies.[17]

---

14 *A New and Impartial Collection of Interesting Letters*, London, 1767, II, 131. *William and Mary College Quarterly*, April 1925, Second Series, 165. *Pennsylvania Evening Post*, May 14, 1776.

15 *Massachusetts Spy*, November 10, 1774. The Virginia planters attempted to prohibit the importation of Negro slaves into the colony largely because they feared that Virginia would cease to be "a white man's country" if the blacks were not kept out.

16 Additional MS. 27382, British Museum, folio 191.

17 *The Interests of the Merchants and Manufacturers of Great Britain in the present Contest with the Colonies Stated and Considered*, London, 1774, 38. This legislation did not entirely suppress colonial paper money. A loophole was

Although this prohibition "hushed the complaints of a few arrogant merchants," it added materially to the burdens of the colonists.[18] The exportation of specie from the mother country to the colonies was not permitted because mercantilism dictated that gold and silver be kept at home — and in consequence a severe money scarcity prevailed in the colonies after 1764. The combination of the lack of a circulating medium and the threat of high taxes helped create the conditions from which the radical spirit in America sprang. It was widely recognized in Great Britain that by virtually stripping the colonies of paper money they had been left in an intolerable position; but Parliament was unable to bring itself to take any steps toward remedying the damage it had wrought. Constructive statesmanship was sadly lacking in the England of George III; and Parliament was content to rest with prohibitions and let Americans find their salvation if they could. Although Benjamin Franklin worked assiduously in England to persuade the government to relieve the money shortage, his arguments made little impression; too often Englishmen acted upon the principle that whatever the friends of the colonies wanted must be wrong and was certainly to the detriment of the mother country.[19]

found in the issuance of treasury notes, which, not being legal tender, were redeemed after a short period by money derived from taxation. Also the notes of loan banks continued to circulate after 1764. About $12,000,000 were in circulation in the colonies in 1774. (Davis Rich Dewey, *Financial History of the United States,* New York, 1931, 29–30.)

[18] *Junius Americanus,* London, 1770, 4–5.

[19] *Pennsylvania Journal and Weekly Advertiser,* September 14, 1769. *Pennsylvania Chronicle,* March 13, 1769. *Colonial Records of North Carolina,* VIII, 10–11; IX, 79. *New York Gazette and Weekly Mercury,* June 4, 1770.

Most of the colonies repeatedly petitioned the British government to relax its restrictions upon paper money. The American merchants were torn between their desire for an adequate supply of money and their fear that if Parliament let the bars down the debtor classes would flood the provinces with depreciated paper money. After 1764, however, the financial stringency became so acute that the merchants were driven to the conclusion that paper money was essential to their prosperity. Specie was quickly drained off to England. The fact that the colonies bought £500,000 of goods from Great Britain and sold only £300,000 in return made it inevitable, as Washington said, that the specie and wealth accumulated by Americans would "centre in Great Britain, as certain as the Needle will settle to the Poles."[20] One of the first acts of Parliament to be overthrown by the American revolutionaries after the calling of the Continental Congress was the prohibition upon paper money. The colonies began to print paper money in 1775; and it was decreed that anyone who refused to accept this or who spoke disrespectfully of it was to be treated as an enemy of the country.

By 1763, it had been made painfully evident to Americans that whenever a colonial commodity became important it was enumerated; and whenever colonial enterprise competed with powerful British interest it was struck down by an act of Parliament. To protect the monopoly of British manufactures, Parliament forbade Americans to export colonial wool, woolens, and hats from one colony to

[20] *The Writings of George Washington,* edited by J. C. Fitzpatrick, Washington, 1931, II, 466. *The Importance of the British Plantations in America to this Kingdom,* London, 1739, 108. *Political Register,* London, 1768, III, 289. *The Scots Magazine,* Edinburgh, 1766, XXVII, 49. *Pennsylvania Chronicle,* July 4, 1768.

another on pain of seizure of ship and cargo; and in 1750 the erection of plating or slitting mills was prohibited. These acts were not part of the Laws of Trade but they were a significant manifestation of mercantilism. They were the work of British manufacturers who believed that colonial manufacturing was responsible for the hard times that had befallen these industries in Old England. Mercantilists warmly espoused the cause of the distressed English manufacturers: the colonists, they contended, must be prevented from rivaling the mother country since the very reason for their existence was to increase her wealth, not to compete with her industries. It is noteworthy, however, that Americans made little protest against these restraints upon their economic freedom. Subservience to unpopular laws merely out of respect for the majesty of the British King and Parliament was never an American characteristic; but so long as there was no effective enforcement of the laws against colonial manufacturing, Americans were not greatly concerned over their existence upon the statute books. Even if the acts had been rigorously enforced, the damage to colonial economy would have been negligible — in contrast to the economy of Ireland, where the destruction of the woolen industry by Parliament did great injury. No important trade in woolens existed in the colonies; and the prohibition of the hat trade and the curtailing of the manufacture of iron and steel utensils did not cause serious distress. These articles could be imported from England as cheaply as they could be manufactured in America and unemployed workers could always be absorbed by agriculture or other trades. Moreover, only a small part of colonial manufacturing came within the purview of these acts of Parliament; and even in

most of the industries affected the colonists were not prohibited from making articles for their own use — it was merely provided that hats, wool, and woolen goods could not be exported from one colony to another. The most important branches of colonial manufacturing were not touched. New England engaged in a considerable traffic with the other colonies in shoes (Lynn, Massachusetts, even in the seventeenth century was a center of shoemaking), soap, candles, coaches, leather goods, chariots, and chaises — but Parliament made no effort to interfere with this trade.

The law of 1750 prohibiting the erection of slitting mills was likewise not regarded as a grievance at the time of its passage. Americans "took no Notice of it as it was insignificant and did not hurt them." The act did not destroy the existing mills; it simply froze the industry, and did no injury to entrepreneurs already in the field. Although the law required American ironmasters to send their iron to England to be slitted and returned to the colonies in manufactured form, they found that they could still enjoy "a Very Pretty Profitt upon it."[21] A far more serious blow was the enumeration of iron in 1767. William Allen of Philadelphia, one of the leading iron producers, declared that his business had been "knocked in the head." He was obliged to shut down half his ironworks and run the remainder at a loss. Most of the forges in Pennsylvania, despite the abundance of cheap ore, were closed or converted into bloomeries. Indeed, the result of this legislation was to make iron manufacturers objects of charity: in 1771,

[21] *The Trade and Navigation of Great Britain Considered,* London, 1730, 80–81. *The Importance of the British Plantations in America to this Kingdom,* London, 1739, 75–77, 107. Additional MS. 33030, folio 117.

Governor John Penn appointed to the customhouse at Philadelphia one Lardner, a bankrupt ironmaster who had lost his fortune, "as," said the governor, "has been the case with most people who of late Years have engaged in that sort of business."[22]

Americans were tardy in discovering the tyranny of these restrictions. It was not until after the passage of the Stamp Act that their real menace was perceived; and then they became rich grist indeed for the propaganda mills of the patriots. "When all this black roll of impositions is view'd together," exclaimed an American in 1776, "what a shocking series of partial, tyrannic oppression do they present."[23] The true significance of these acts lies in their effect not so much upon colonial economy as upon colonial psychology: they helped to establish the conviction in the minds of many Americans that Great Britain regarded the growth of the colonies with implacable jealousy and hostility. She seemed determined to check their progress lest they grow too strong for her control; therefore, exclaimed an American, she had adopted this "Ottoman policy, by strangling us in infancy."[24] So "jealous of our rising Glory" did Great Britain appear that the colonists began to believe that "if the extent of our commerce should draw into our hands the wealth of all the Indies," Parliament would "provide ways and means for conveying the whole into the treasury of England" — leaving Americans to find "another vacant world" beyond the reach of British authority. These evils, it is true, were merely in the breeze, but they were not for that reason less real to Americans after 1765. Charles Carroll of Carrollton believed that the British government might prohibit all household manufactures in America. "Ye severity of ye weather," said Carroll, "would pinch to death thousands of poor naked Americans. . . . England would then have nothing to fear from our numbers."[25] Carroll regarded the acts restraining colonial manufacturing as more inimical than the Stamp Act itself; they opened the door for illimitable oppression by Parliament and might be converted into a dangerous form of taxation. "If I am to be fleeced, an American might say," remarked Carroll, "if my money is to be taken from me without my consent, it is immaterial to me what manner this is effected."[26] Carroll's fears were shared by George Washington and other Virginians who believed that Virginia could never become a great center of manufacturing as long as this threat of annihilation by act of Parliament hung over the head of colonial enterprise.[27]

These restraints upon American economic liberty revealed, moreover, that a

22 A. C. Bining, *Pennsylvania Iron Manufacture in the Eighteenth Century*, Publications of the Pennsylvania Historical Commission, Harrisburg, IV, 38. William Allen to Thomas Penn, September 23, 1768, and October 8, 1767; John Penn to Henry Wilmot, January ?, 1771, Penn. MSS., *Official Correspondence*, X, Historical Society of Pennsylvania.

23 *Pennsylvania Packet*, May 13, 1776.

24 *Political Register*, London, 1768, II, 289, 292. Reverend Jacob Duché, *The Duty of Standing Fast in our Spiritual and Temporal Liberties*, Philadelphia, 1775, 15.

25 *The Life and Correspondence of Joseph Reed*, edited by William B. Reed, Philadelphia, 1847, I, 31. *Unpublished Letters of Charles Carroll of Carrollton*, edited by T. M. Field. The U. S. Catholic Historical Society, Monographs, Series I, New York, 1902, 139–140; 148–149.

26 *Ibid.*, 139–140.

27 *The Writings of George Washington*, edited by John C. Fitzpatrick, II, 502. *Virginia Gazette* (Rind's), July 6, 1769. *Providence Gazette and Country Journal*, March 12, 1766. *Pennsylvania Gazette*, February 22, 1775. *Boston Gazette*, April 29, 1765. *An Appeal to the Justice and Interest of the People of Great Britain in the present Disputes with America*. By an old Member of Parliament, London, 1776, 37.

handful of English capitalists carried more weight at Westminster than the welfare of millions of Americans. "A colonist cannot make a button, horse-shoe, nor a hob-nail," exclaimed a Bostonian, "but some sooty ironmonger or respectable button-maker of Britain shall bawl and squal that his honors worship is most egregiously maltreated, injured, cheated and robb'd by the rascally American republicans."[28] "Britain," said Benjamin Franklin, "would, if she could, manufacture & trade for all the World; — England for all Britain; — London for all England; — and every Londoner for all London." Englishmen were given American soil and mines, and sometimes they refused, as in the case of the Louisbourg coal mines, either to develop them or to allow Americans to do so. By this means, it was contended, the British government made "an abridgment of the common bounties of Heaven"; "the water is not permitted to flow, or the earth to produce," lamented a colonist, "for the same beneficial purposes to the American as for the Briton."[29]

Thus these laws, in the hands of American propagandists, helped to establish the conviction that imperial policy was being perverted to the enrichment of British monopolists. Americans seemed to be the sheep and British merchants and manufacturers the shearers. The colonists were not easily reconciled to exploitation: they did not believe that God had intended the American continent to be the property of English "merchant tailors and woolen drapers" nor was it ordained that Englishmen should have

an "indefeasable right to the agonies, toils, and bloody sweat of the inhabitants of this land, and to the profits and products of all their labors."[30] Parliament had no right to "crush their native talents and to keep them in a constant state of inferiority."[31] Rather, God and nature had decreed that America was to be a "Great Empire" and the center of the arts and sciences. From this point of view, British efforts to prevent Americans from fully utilizing the riches with which nature had endowed them were an attempt to thwart God's plans for the Western Hemisphere.

It cannot be denied that there was widespread discontent among the colonists, particularly among the Southern planters, with the workings of British mercantilism. Certainly, they regarded a larger measure of economic freedom as one of the most desirable results of the revolutionary agitation of 1765–1776. The closing of certain channels of trade essential to the well-being of the Northern colonies and the efforts of the mother country to enforce the Acts of Trade after 1764 brought Northern merchants to see British mercantilism eye to eye with the Southern tobacco growers. In the correspondence of colonial merchants and planters there is a growing volume of complaint that they were risking their capital and expending their energy for the enrichment of British merchants and manufacturers. They chafed under a system which bottled up initiative and confined trade to channels prescribed by the British government, which, as was well known, frequently acted at the behest of powerful British commercial and manufacturing interests. We shall find that as

[28] *Boston Gazette*, April 29, 1765. *Virginia Gazette*, December 3, 1772.

[29] *The Writings of Benjamin Franklin*, edited by A. H. Smyth, New York, 1906, IV, 244–245. *Pennsylvania Gazette*, February 22, 1775. Ramsay, I, 62.

[30] *Boston Gazette*, April 29, 1765.

[31] *Pennsylvania Packet and General Advertiser*, July 4, 1774.

Americans progressively enlarged their demands for liberty after 1765, the Acts of Trade and the entire system of British mercantilism came to be included within their definition of tyranny. Without doubt, underlying the resounding phrases and ideals of the American Revolution, there was a solid foundation of economic grievances which played an important part in determining the course taken by both the Northern merchants and the Southern planters.

Yet it cannot be said that Americans were driven to rebellion by intolerable economic oppression. In general, after the postwar depression of 1763–1765, the revolutionary period was an era of growth and prosperity for the colonies. The British "tyranny" against which Americans rebelled did little to impede their material development; on the contrary, the population continued to double every generation by natural means and the demand for British manufactures increased apace. In many New England towns it was difficult to find a man not in easy circumstances. The colonial seaports continued to hum with business: in 1762 New York had 477 vessels; by 1772, the number had increased to 709.[32]

The immediate threat to American liberty and well-being after 1765 came not from the restrictions imposed upon colonial trade and manufacturing but from Parliament's efforts to raise a revenue in the colonies. It was the invasion of Americans' political rights by Parliament after the Peace of Paris which precipitated the struggle between the mother country and colonies and inspired the ideals and slogans of the American Revolution. Economic grievances played a secondary part in the patriots' propaganda; from 1765 to 1776, political issues were kept uppermost. This was in accord with the tenor of American history. Throughout the colonial period, the rights and privileges of the assemblies were regarded as the first line of defense of American liberty, both political and economic. If they were overthrown, the colonists believed themselves destined to become as "errant slaves as any in Turkey." Thus, so long as the colonists remained British subjects, they threw their full strength into the struggle to maintain the rights of their assemblies, firmly convinced that the success or failure of their efforts would determine whether liberty or slavery was to prevail in America.

[32] David Ramsay, *The History of the Revolution in South Carolina*, Trenton, 1785, I, 7–8. *Documents relative to the Colonial History of the State of New York*, Albany, 1857, VIII, 446.

Carl Becker: THE SPIRIT OF '76

*Last October Mr. Lyon asked me to come down to the Brookings School
and tell you about the Spirit of '76. I suspected that he hadn't any clear
notion of what was meant by the phrase "Spirit of '76," and I was positive
I hadn't. I was therefore about to decline the invitation when, rummaging
among my papers, I came upon an old and imperfect manuscript which
seemed providentially designed to throw some light on this obscure subject. The manuscript bore the date of 1792, but who may have written it
I was unable to determine. There are obviously some pages missing, and
the tale ends suddenly as if never quite finished. But such as it is I have
transcribed it, and I give it to you for what it may be worth. The title of
the manuscript is "Jeremiah Wynkoop."*

JEREMIAH WYNKOOP

DURING the war of independence I
not infrequently heard zealous patriots say that Mr. Wynkoop was not
as warm in the cause as he should be.
The charge has lately been revived by
those who had no great liking for Mr.
Wynkoop's Federalist principles. Mr.
Wynkoop was of course not alone in
being thus distinguished. It is now said
of many men who were never suspected
of being Tory that they look back with
regret to the old days before the breach
with Britain. It is said of them, to employ a phrase now becoming current,
that they were never really inspired by
the true spirit of '76. For my part, I sus-
pect that, in recalling the desperate days
of the war, we are likely to invest the
so-called spirit of '76 with a glamor which
it did not have at the time. Be that as
it may, I knew Jeremiah Wynkoop as an
honest man and a genuine patriot. I was
his closest friend, intimate enough to
know better than most the difficulties

that confronted him and the sentiments
that determined his conduct. And so I
think it worth while, now that the man
is dead, to set down a plain tale of his
activities and opinions from the beginning of the quarrel in 1763 to the final
breach in 1776. This I do, not only for
old friendship's sake and as a justification
of Mr. Wynkoop, but as a contribution
to the history of those troubled times;
for Jeremiah Wynkoop was fairly
representative, both in his station in life
and in his opinions, of that considerable
class of substantial men who did as much
as any other class, and I think more than
any other class, to enable these states to
maintain their liberties against British
tyranny.

Born of rich middle class parents of
genuine Dutch-American stock, Jeremiah
was educated at Kings College, then recently established. In fact we both
entered the College the year it was
founded, and graduated with the first

class in 1758. Jeremiah then spent two years in the office of William Moore reading law, a profession which he nevertheless abandoned for the trade. Taking over a profitable business upon the sudden death of his father, he rapidly achieved a notable success in commerce, chiefly in West Indian ventures, and was already known, in 1765, as a leading merchant in New York, where he had offices near the wharves, and a town house, inherited from his father, on the Bowling Green. But Jeremiah, being much given to study and the reading of books, preferred to live away from the distractions of the city, and had in fact for some years resided in the country, out Greenwich Village way, where he possessed a fine estate which had come to him as part of the generous dowry of his wife, the daughter of old Nicholas Van Schoickendinck, a great landowner in the province.

Mr. Wynkoop was much given to the reading of books, as I have said; and it is necessary to dwell on this matter a little since it helps to explain his opinions and conduct. Of all books, histories of the ancient and the modern times were his favorite study. It was an interest which he acquired in college, and never afterward lost. In college of course we all read the standard Greek and Roman writers, and acquired the usual knowledge of classical history. To admire the classical poets and essayists was nothing out of the way for young men in college, but the ancient civilization fascinated Jeremiah more than most of us, and I recall that he devoured every book on that subject which the college afforded, and many others which he bought or borrowed. The Parallel Lives of Plutarch he knew almost by heart, and was never weary of discanting on the austere morality and virtuous republicanism of those heroic times. For Jeremiah a kind of

golden age was pictured there, a lost world which forever disappeared when Caesar crossed the Rubicon. The later Roman times never interested him much — "five hundred years," he used to say, "in which the civilized world groaned under the heavy hands of tyrants, relieved only by the reigns of five good emperors." Still less was he interested in the Dark Ages, when the light of learning and the spirit of liberty were submerged by feudal anarchy and ecclesiastical superstition. But the story of modern times fascinated Jeremiah as much as the story of the ancient world because all its significance seemed to lie in the slow and painful emergence from that long mediaeval night, through the recovery of the wisdom of the ancients, the progress of natural philosophy, and the struggle fo. political liberty.

All these matters I recall we used to discuss at great length, so that I was perfectly familiar with Jeremiah's reflections on history. At that time his ideas seemed to me wonderfully novel and interesting, but I have since thought them, in a vague general way at least, those of most cultivated Americans. Be that as it may, all the significance of history appeared to Mr. Wynkoop to lie in the age-long conflict between Truth and Error, between Freedom and Oppression. And for this reason he opined that the central event of modern times was the struggle of the last century between the English people and the Stuart kings. With the history of that heroic time he was entirely familiar, and in a less degree I was too. Our heroes were Pym and Eliot, and John Hampden, imprisoned for refusing to pay a twenty shilling tax. Cromwell we admired as the man of iron who had forever laid the ghost of the Divine Right doctrine, and whose mistakes were later corrected by the liberal Whigs who called in Dutch William to replace the last of the Stuarts. We knew the great charters of liberty — the Magna Charta, the Petition of Right and the Bill of Rights. We knew our Milton, the man who defended the authority of elected magistrates, and erected an impregnable bulwark against the denial of free speech. We knew our Grotius, who had discovered in right reason the foundation of civil and international society. Above all we knew our Locke, and especially his second discourse on Civil Government, in which he so eloquently defended the Revolution of '88 as an act of reasonable men defending their natural rights against the usurping king who had broken the original compact.

Much as Jeremiah admired England as the home of political liberty, he was thoroughly American, and it was always his idea that America had played a most notable part in the great modern struggle against the oppression of Church and State. He used to find great satisfaction in recalling that our ancestors, at the hazard of their lives and fortunes, had braved the terrors of the new world in pursuit of religious and political liberty; that they had persisted, often at the point of failure, in the desperate determination to transform the inhospitable wilderness into a land fit for human habitation; and he would point out that they had succeeded beyond any reasonable expectation, so much so that these thirteen colonies were now the most fortunate and the freest countries in the world — thirteen communities living in peace and content, happily without kings, neither burdened with an idle aristocracy nor menaced by a depraved populace, with a press uncensored, and many religious faiths deprived of the power of persecution and long habituated to the spirit of toleration. For my part I used to com-

plain sometimes that after all we were only "provincials," remote from the center of things. I used to express the wish that fate had set us down in London, nearer Piccadilly and the Beefsteak Club. But Jeremiah would have none of such repining. Provincials we might be in a geographical sense, he would say, but spiritually we were at "the center of the world, in the direct line of those heroes and martyrs who since the beginning of time have done battle for the dignity and happiness of mankind against the leagued assailants of both."

Here some pages are missing in the manuscript. It goes on as follows.

". . . are become so populous and wealthy that we are as indispensable to Britain as Britain is to us. The time is surely approaching when this vast country will be the center of power and wealth of the Empire. We are now freed from the French menace. The peace will be an enduring one, and the two branches of the English race will continue in the future as in the past to exemplify to the world those incomparable blessings that are the prerogatives of free peoples."

Such was Jeremiah Wynkoop's conception of history in general and of the part which Britain and America had played in the story of human progress. With him it was a kind of philosophy, a religion indeed, the only religion really that he had. I don't mean that he was of the atheistical school of thought. He believed indeed in the existence of the Deity as the First Cause and Original Contriver of the universe; and this was in fact the very reason why he found so much delight in the study of history. History was God's revelation of the meaning of life and of human destiny on earth, making plain the gradual progress and the ultimate triumph of Truth and Freedom. And this I think was the secret of his profound loyalty to both Britain and America; these were in his view the promised lands, the homes of the chosen peoples whose mission it was to lead mankind toward the final goal.

Nothing at all events was farther from his thought in 1763 than that there could be any serious differences between the two peoples who were so bound together by ties of blood and affection, by mutual respect, and by the common tradition of. . .

Another break in the manuscript here.

In the year 1765 Mr. Wynkoop shared the general feeling of apprehension which for two years had been steadily increasing on account of the measures, as unprecedented as they were unfortunate, of the king's minister, Mr. George Grenville. The chief of these measures were undoubtedly the Sugar Act of the last, and the Stamp Act of the then present year. On the nature and effects of these measures Mr. Wynkoop had read and reflected as much as a busy man well could do. The Sugar Act, obviously designed to placate the British West Indian sugar planters, was certain, as indeed it was intended, to put obstacles in the way of the island trade with New York and New England. In that trade Mr. Wynkoop was personally interested. It is true, as indeed he was careful to tell me, that his profits for the last year were much as usual; but it had been abundantly demonstrated in pamphlets that the Sugar duties were bound to have a disastrous effect on American trade in general; would, for example, undermine the New England rum industry and thereby depress the fisheries and the African trade; would diminish the exports of lumber

and grain from New York and Pennsylvania; would above all, since the new duties were to be paid in silver, drain the colonies of their small store of hard money and thereby make it difficult for American merchants to settle their balances due in London on account of imported British manufactures.

No one doubted, at least no one in America, that the Sugar Act was unwise in point of policy, calculated to defeat the very end intended. Yet there it was, an act of Parliament imposing duties for the regulation of trade, and we could not deny that Parliament had long exercised without opposition the right to regulate trade. But I recall Mr. Wynkoop's pointing out to me one novel feature of the act, which was the declared purpose, expressed in the preamble, of raising a revenue in "his Majesty's dominions in America, for defraying the expenses of defending, protecting, and securing the same." For some reason Mr. Wynkoop disliked the term "dominions," always preferring the term "colonies." But he disliked still more the term "securing." For two years ministers had been prone to talk of laying restrictions on his Majesty's dominions for their better security. This idea Mr. Wynkoop disliked extremely. I remember his saying that the term "free-born Englishmen" had always given him great satisfaction, that he had always supposed that Americans were possessed of all the rights of Englishmen born within the realm; and indeed I knew him well enough to know that he harbored the firm conviction that Americans were not only as free as Englishmen but even a little freer, a degree less subservient to aristocrats and kings, a degree more emancipated from custom and the dead hand of the past. I often heard him compare the Assembly of New York, chosen by the free suffrages of the people, with the British Parliament in which so often the members were chosen by irresponsible Peers and Boroughmongers — compare them of course to the disadvantage of the latter. To suppose that Parliament was now bent upon restricting the dearly bought and well deserved liberties of America was to Jeremiah, as indeed it was to all of us, an alien and distressing thought.

We could scarcely therefore avoid asking the question: "What constitutional right has the British Parliament to legislate in restraint of American liberties?" We never doubted that we were possessed of liberties, and no American, certainly no American as well informed as Mr. Wynkoop, needed to be told that there was a British Constitution which guaranteed the rights of Englishmen. Yet, as I recall those early years, I must confess that we were somewhat perplexed, had a little the air of groping about in the dark for the precise provisions of the British Constitution. The spirit of the British Constitution we knew was to be found in the Magna Charta and the Bill of Rights. Rights were indeed of its very essence; and to Mr. Wynkoop at least it was incredible that there was not to be found in it an adequate guarantee of the rights which Americans ought to enjoy. I remember his reading to me certain passages from the pamphlets of Stephen Hopkins and Governor Hutchinson — pamphlets which he thought expressed the American view very adequately. "What motive," Mr. Hopkins asked, "can remain to induce the Parliament to hedge the principles and lessen the rights of the most dutiful and loyal subjects — subjects justly entitled to ample freedom, who have long enjoyed and not abused, their liberties?" This passage I think expressed Mr. Wynkoop's state of mind very well in the year

of the Sugar Act. His state of mind was one of amazement, the state of mind of a man who is still at the point of asking questions — Why? For what reason?

Meantime the Stamp Act, presenting the question more clearly, did much to clarify our ideas on the matter of American taxation; and certainly Mr. Wynkoop was never in doubt as to the unconstitutionality of that famous measure. In those days I was much at Mr. Wynkoop's house, and I remember one day in November, 1765, sitting with him and his father-in-law, old Nicholas Van Schoickendinck, discussing the state of the nation. Even old Nicholas had been startled out of his customary complacency by the furious excitement occasioned by the Stamp Act.

"The Act is unconstitutional, sir," Mr. Wynkoop had just declared, somewhat dogmatically it must be confessed, and for perhaps the third time. "There can be no question about that I think. It is not only contrary to precedent, but is destructive of British liberty, the fundamental principle of which is that Englishmen may not be taxed without their own consent. We certainly never gave our assent to the Stamp Act."

"I won't say no to that," old Nicholas remarked. "And if we had done no more than to protest the measure I should be well content."

"Little good protests would have done, sir. We protested before the bill was passed, and without effect. Mr. Grenville would not hear our protests, and now he finds the act virtually nullified. I can't say I regret it."

"Nullified!" Old Nicholas exclaimed with some asperity. "A soft word for a nasty business. Mr. Grenville finds his law 'nullified,' you say. But in getting the law nullified we get half the windows of the Broad Way smashed too, and Governor Colden gets his chariot burned. For my part I don't know what Mr. Colden's chariot had to do with the devilish stamps — it wasn't designed to carry them."

"Very true, sir, I admit. And regrettable enough, all this parading and disturbance. But if Ministers will play with oppression the people will play with violence. Similar incidents occurred in England itself in the last century. Let Mr. Grenville beware of playing the role of Strafford. God knows I am no friend of rioting. I have windows too. But a little rioting may be necessary on occasion to warn ministers that legislative lawlessness is likely to be met by popular violence."

Mr. Wynkoop had perhaps a little the air of talking to convince himself rather than old Nicholas. Old Nicholas at least was not convinced.

"Tush!" he exclaimed irritably. "That's a new word, 'popular.' You young fellows have picked up a lot of precious democratical phrases, I must say. Who are 'the people' you talk so loosely about? Another word for 'populace' or I miss my guess. Don't delude yourself by supposing that it was hatred of the Stamps that made them break Mr. Livingston's windows and burn Mr. Colden's chariot. They hate Mr. Livingston and Mr. Colden because they are men of substance and standing. It is not windows they aim at but class privileges, the privileges of my class and yours, the class that always has, and I trust always will, govern this province. The bald fact is that a mob of mechanics and ne'er-do-wells, led by obscure fellows like John Lamb and Isaac Sears who have hitherto doffed their caps and known their places, are now aiming to control the city through their self constituted committees. Sons of Liberty, they call themselves; sons of anarchy, in fact. I wish as much as you to preserve our liberties. But I warn you that liberty is a sword that cuts two ways, and if you can't defend your rights against ministerial oppression without stirring the 'people,' you will soon be confronted with the necessity of defending your privileges against the encroachments of the mob on the Bowling Green."

Old Nicholas stopped to light his pipe, and after a few puffs added:

"You don't associate with Mr. John Lamb, do you? You ain't one of the Liberty Boys who erect poles and break windows, I hope."

Mr. Wynkoop laughed off the sarcasm. "Certainly not, sir. I don't know the fellow Lamb, never saw him in fact, although I am told, and believe, that he is an honest, worthy man. The danger you mention has of course occurred to me, but I think you probably exaggerate it. Let Britain repeal the Stamp Act, as she must do, and the populace will be quiet enough."

We sat until a late hour. I took but little part in the discussion, enjoying nothing better than to listen to the good natured wrangling of these two friends. During the course of the evening each repeated, many times over, his former argument, all without rancor, but all equally without effect. Except in opinion, they were not divided; and at last, pledging one another courteously in a glass of stiff toddy, we separated for the night.

During the following months Mr. Wynkoop continued firm in the defence of American rights. He agreed, as all the substantial merchants did, not to use the stamps, which was indeed not possible since none were to be had. Yet he would do no business without them. Let the courts close, he said. Let his ships stand idle in harbor, a year, two years, let them rot there rather than submit to an unconstitutional measure. So I often heard him declare roundly, sitting at dinner sipping his madeira. . . .

Again something missing from the manuscript.

. . . secret misgivings, during the long cold winter, by the continued disturbances in the streets, and by the clamor of those, mostly of the common sort, who demanded that the courts should open and denounced the merchants for timidly refusing to do business without stamps. The Sons of Liberty were saying that the stopping of business was all very well for gentlemen of fortune, but that it was ruining the people who must starve unless business went on as usual. The Sons of Liberty were grown more hostile to the merchants than they were to ministers, and they even hinted that the better sort were by their timidity betraying the cause. Meantime Old Nicholas appeared to enjoy the situation, and never lost an opportunity of asking him, Jeremiah Wynkoop, whether he hadn't yet joined the Liberty Boys, and why after all he didn't send his ships out, clearance papers or no clearance papers.

Mr. Wynkoop was therefore immensely relieved when the British Parliament finally repealed the hateful measure, thus at once justifying his conduct and restoring his confidence in the essential justice of Britain. He had now, I recall, rather the better of the argument with Old Nicholas (the two were forever disputing) and pointed out to him ever so often that a little firmness on America's part was all that was needful to the preservation of her liberties. For two years he went about his business and pleasure with immense content. I dare say he easily forgot, as men will do, the distasteful incidents of the Stamp Act struggle, and allowed his mind to dwell chiefly on its satisfactions. He often spoke of the principle, "No taxation without representation," as being now fully established; often expressed his gratification that, by taking a firm and sensible stand, he and his substantial friends had brought Britain to recognize this principle; so that by the mere passing of time as it were these ideas acquired for Jeremiah a certain axiomatic character. I was never so sure of all this, and sometimes called his attention to the Declaratory Act as evidence that Britain still claimed the right of binding the colonies in all matters whatsoever. Needless to say, old Nicholas called his attention to the Declaratory Act oftener than I did. But Mr. Wynkoop would not take the Declaratory Act seriously. It was, he said, no more than a bravely flying banner designed to cover a dignified retreat from an untenable position; and he had no fear that Britain, having confessed its error by repealing the Stamp Act, would ever again repeat it.

It presently appeared that the British government could commit errors without repeating itself. In 1767, following the mysterious retirement and delphic silences of Mr. Pitt, Mr. Charles Townshend had come forward, no one knew on whose authority, and promised the House to obtain a revenue from America without doing violence to her alleged rights. The Americans, he said, had drawn a distinction between "internal" and "external" taxes, denying the former but admitting the latter. This distinction Mr. Townshend thought "perfect nonsense," but was willing to humor Americans in it; which he would do by laying an external tax on the importation of glass, lead, paper, and tea. These duties, which would bring into the Exchequer about £40,000, the Americans must on their own principles, Mr. Townshend thought, admit to be constitutional.

It may strike my readers as odd that any one could have been surprised by anything Mr. Townshend took a notion to; but we were indeed not then as well aware of the man's essential frivolity as we have since become. I recall at all events that Mr. Wynkoop followed the proceedings in the House with amazement; and when we learned, one day in 1768, that Mr. Townshend had actually blarneyed the House into passing the Tea Act, the whole business struck Jeremiah as preposterous —"doubtless one of those deplorable jokes," I remember his saying, "which Mr. Townshend is fond of perpetrating when half drunk." I had some recollection that in the time of the Stamp Act troubles certain writers had hinted at a distinction between "internal" and "external" taxes; and Mr. Wynkoop admitted that some such distinction may have been made. But he said that for his part he thought little of such subtle distinctions, agreeing rather with Mr. Pitt that the real question was whether Parliament could "take money out of our pockets without our consent" by any tax whatsover. There was, however, a difficulty in taking so advanced a position at that time, and as usual it was old Nicholas, always quick to perceive difficulties, who pointed it out.

"I fancy," old Nicholas had said, "that every act in regulation of trade takes money out of our pockets, but I don't imagine you have yet become so ardent a Son of Liberty as to deny Parliament the right of regulating our trade."

At that time we were all reading Mr. Dickinson's Letters of A Pennsylvania Farmer, and Mr. Wynkoop, who read everything, was able to meet that objection.

"The essential question," he said, "is whether an act of Parliament is laid primarily for the regulation of trade or for the raising of a revenue. If for the latter, it is a tax. The intention of the framers must decide, and there can be no question that the Tea Act is a tax since the framers expressly declare its purpose to be the raising of a revenue."

"A fine distinction, that! But it would be easy for the framers of an act to levy duties on imports with the real intention of raising a revenue, all the while professing loudly their intention of regulating trade. What then?"

"Americans would not be so easily deceived, sir. The nature of the Act would reveal the real intention clearly enough."

"Ha! You would determine the nature of an act by the intention of the framers, and the intention of the framers by the nature of the act. Excellent! That is the logic of your Pennsylvania Farmer. The New Englanders are still more advanced, I see. They are now saying that our rights are founded on a law of Nature, and God only knows what that is. God and Mr. Adams — it's the same thing, I dare say."

"The New Englanders are likely to be a little rash, sir, I think," Mr. Wynkoop admitted. "The argument of their Mr. Adams is complicated, and I fear too subtle to be easily followed. I'm not sure I understand it."

"Well, never mind. You will all understand it soon enough. First you say that Britain has no right to lay internal taxes. Then that she has no right to levy taxes of any sort. Next you will be saying that Parliament has no right of legislation for the colonies on any matter whatsoever. And as you can't derive that from precedent you will derive it from the law of nature."

Mr. Wynkoop smiled at this outburst.

"I have no fear of its coming to that," he said. "The Tea Act is not really an act of Britain; it is Mr. Townshend's foolish hobby. A firm and sensible resistance on our part will effect its repeal. But if one could conceive Britain to be so blind as to push matters to extremes — well, I don't know. If it were really a choice between admitting that Parliament has a right of making all laws for us or denying that she has a right of making any laws for us, it would be a hard choice, but should we not be forced to choose the latter alternative? What other answer could we make?"

"You may well ask! What answer will you make when your precious Adams comes out with a declaration of independency from Great Britain?"

"Independence!" Mr. Wynkoop exclaimed. "Good God, sir, what an idea!"

And indeed, at that time, the idea of separation from Great Britain struck us all as fantastic.

A firm and sensible resistance, Jeremiah had maintained, would bring a repeal of the Townshend duties, as it had formerly brought a repeal of the Stamp Act. When it was learned that Lord North, on March 5, 1770, had moved the repeal of all the Townshend duties save that on tea, Mr. Wynkoop could with some reason say, and did say, that events had proved the justice of his view. And Mr. Wynkoop felt, rightly enough, although he modestly refrained from boasting of it, that he had contributed to this happy result. With no more than the grudging consent of old Nicholas, he had taken a leading part in organizing the Merchant's Association — an agreement not to import any goods from Great Britain so long as the Townshend duties should be in force. That Association had been faithfully kept by the New York merchants of substance and standing.

Mr. Wynkoop had himself kept it to the letter, and had sacrificed much in doing so. He told me that his enlarged stock of goods, ordered in anticipation of the agreement, had soon been sold out — at high prices indeed, but not sufficiently high to recoup him for his subsequent losses. For four months last past business had been dull beyond all precedent — scarcely a ship moving; debts not to be collected; money hardly to be had at any price; and the poorer sort of people in dire need for want of employment.

There were indeed plenty of unscrupulous men who had done well enough, who had even profited while pretending to defend their country's rights. The Boston and Philadelphia merchants, as was definitely known in New York, had observed the Association none too well; and even in New York men of no standing had done a thriving business in the smuggling way, especially in Holland tea. Obviously the longer the Association was maintained by honest merchants, the more unscrupulous smugglers would profit by it. We were therefore somewhat surprised to learn that the Boston merchants were in favor of maintaining the Association in full vigor, in spite of Lord North's concessions, so long as the 3d duty on tea was retained. This policy was also advocated by the dishonest beneficiaries of the system in New York, who made use of agitators like Mr. Mac-Dougall to stir up the Mechanics Association and the populace generally against the Merchants, their argument being that our liberties were as much endangered by the 3d duty on tea as they had been by all the Townshend duties.

I am not so sure now that they were wrong, but at that time all of the substantial merchants of New York were strong for a modification of the Association. Mr. Wynkoop, I recall, took a leading part in the affair. He was much irritated with the Boston merchants whom he described as being more active in "resolving what to do than in doing what they had resolved." His opinion was that the Association no longer served any "purpose other than to tie the hands of honest men to let rogues, smugglers, and men of no character plunder their country." Besides, he was much gratified, as all the merchants were, by the recent act of the British government permitting the issue in New York of a paper currency, which was so essential to business prosperity. And therefore, in view of the fact that Britain had taken the first step by repealing the major part of the Townshend duties, it seemed to him the part of wisdom for the colonies to make some concession on their part. The New York merchants of standing were I think generally of Mr. Wynkoop's opinion; and at all events, after taking a canvass of the city, they resolved to abandon the old Association, agreeing for the future to import all commodities, "except teas and other articles that are or may be subject to an importation duty." Some were apprehensive lest New York might find itself alone in this action, and thereby suffer the stigma of having deserted the cause. But in the event it proved otherwise, as Mr. Wynkoop had anticipated. In spite of protests from Boston and Philadelphia, the merchants of those cities followed the lead of New York. Demonstrations in the streets soon subsided, importation became general, business revived, and the controversy with Britain seemed definitely closed.

The years of '71 and '72 were quiet years — ominously so as it proved. But in those days we all nourished the conviction that the controversy with Britain was definitely closed. Nothing occurred to remind us of it even, unless it would be the annual celebrations of the repeal of the Stamp Act, or the faint reverberations, always to be heard in any case, of political squabbles in the Massachusetts Bay. Then, out of a clear sky as it seemed, the storm burst — the landing of the tea ships, the destruction of the tea in Boston harbor, and the subsequent meeting of the Philadelphia Congress. These events, all occurring in rapid succession, seemed to fall like so many blows on Mr. Wynkoop's head, and I recall his saying to me. . . .

Here the manuscript breaks off again, and there are evidently some pages missing.

. . . return from Philadelphia, I met him at his father's house where we were to take dinner, as often happened. Arriving early, we had a long talk while waiting for old Nicholas to come down. I found Mr. Wynkoop in low spirits, an unusual thing for him. It may have been no more than a natural weakness after the excitement of attending the Congress, but to my accustomed eyes his low spirits seemed rather due to the uncomfortable feeling that he had been elbowed by circumstances into a position which he never intended to occupy. I was eager for the details of the Congress, but he seemed unwilling to talk of that, preferring rather to dwell upon the events leading up to it — matters which we had threshed out many times before. It was as if Mr. Wynkoop wished to revive the events of the last year and his own part in them, as if, feeling that he might and perhaps should have followed a different line of conduct, his mind was eagerly engaged in finding some good reasons for the line of conduct which he had followed in fact. What first gave me this notion was his saying, *apropos* of nothing.

"I will confess to you, what I would not to another, that if I could twelve months ago have foreseen the present situation I should probably not have attended the Congress."

The remark alarmed me. Mr. Wynkoop's admiration for Britain and his faith in her essential justice were always stronger than mine. For my part I doubted not, from the moment of the passing of the Coercive Acts, that we were in for it, that Britain would not back down again, and that we must either break with her or submit to her demands. My decision was made. I would go with America when the time came for the final breach, I knew that; and above all things I wished Mr. Wynkoop, who was my closest friend, to throw the weight of his powerful interest on the side of my country. But I knew him well enough to be sure that if he now convinced himself that it would come to a breach with Britain he would probably wash his hands of the whole business. What I counted on was a certain capacity in the man, I won't say for deceiving himself, but for convincing himself that what he strongly desired would somehow come to pass. I therefore did what I could to convince him, or rather to help him convince himself, that his past and present conduct was that of a wise and prudent man.

"No man can foresee the future," I remarked, somewhat sententiously.

"That is true," he said. "And even could I have foreseen the future, I fail to see how I could have acted differently, at least not honorably and with any satisfaction to myself. It is past a doubt that Britain, in authorizing the India Company to sell its teas in America, deliberately sought to raise the issue with America once more. It was a challenge, and so insidiously contrived that America had

no choice but submission or a resort to a certain amount of violence. Once landed the teas were bound to be sold, since even with the 3d duty they were offered at a less price than the Holland teas. The issue could not be met by commercial agreements, still less by argument. Well, we sent the teas back to London. The Massachusetts people threw theirs into the harbor. Violence, undoubtedly. I had no part in it, but what could be done? Who after all was responsible for the violence? Let ministers who revived an issue happily settled answer that."

"There is no doubt in my mind," I said, "that Britain welcomed the violence in Boston harbor as a pretext for strong measures."

"It seems incredible," Mr. Wynkoop resumed, "but what else can we think? Hitherto it might be said of ministers that they blundered, that they did not know the consequences of their acts. But not on this occasion. They knew perfectly the temper of America; and in any case the destruction of a little tea was surely a mild offense compared with the abrogation of the Massachusetts Charter and the closing of Boston harbor. To subject a loyal province to military despotism, and then deliberately to set about starving the people into submission reveals a vindictiveness foreign to the British character. I can't think the Coercive Acts represent the will of the English people, and I am confident, always have been, that the sober second thought of the nation will repudiate these acts of ministerial despotism."

It was not the first time I had heard Mr. Wynkoop express that sentiment.

"I trust it may prove so," I said. "At least we have done our part. No one can say that the Congress has countenanced rash measures. It has merely adopted a commercial agreement, a measure which we have frequently resorted to before. I don't see how it could have done less."

Mr. Wynkoop seemed a little uncertain of that.

"Yes," he said. "I suppose we could not have done less; Heaven knows we have shown a proper restraint. And I may say that what little influence I have had has always been exerted to that end."

I knew well enough what he was thinking of. After the tea episode there were rash spirits who talked of resort to arms, and even hinted at independence. There were such men even in New York. They had formed the Committee of 25, but fortunately the more moderate minded had got the committee enlarged to 51; and Mr. Wynkoop, together with Mr. Jay and Mr. Alsop and other men of substance, had consented to serve on the Committee of 51 in order to prevent the firebrands from carrying the province into violent measures. Old Nicholas had advised against it.

"Beware of meddling with treason," I recall hearing him say to Mr. Wynkoop at that time.

"Precisely my idea," Mr. Wynkoop had replied, with the smile he always had for old Nicholas' penchant for using stronger terms than the occasion warranted. "I wish to steer clear of treason, or anything remotely approaching it. But it is plain to be seen that New York will support Boston in some fashion, plain to be seen that she will send delegates to Philadelphia. Suppose I and all moderate men follow your advice and wash our hands of the affair? What then? Then the Mechanics will take the lead and send MacDougall and Sears and men of their kidney to Philadelphia, with instructions for vigorous measures. Vigorous measures! God only knows what measures they may be for!"

It was to keep New York from violent measures of all sorts that Mr. Wynkoop had consented to serve on the Committee of 51; it was for that reason he had gone to Philadelphia. I knew that better than most, and I knew that that was what he was now thinking of.

"I am very glad you went to Philadelphia," I said.

"What else could I have done?" he exclaimed. "I have asked myself that a dozen times without finding any answer. But about the Association I don't know. You say it is a moderate measure, but after all it was the measure of the New Englanders, and among the moderates of Philadelphia it was commonly thought to be perhaps too vigorous. I was opposed to it. I voted against it. And having done so perhaps I was ill advised to sign it. I don't know."

I was about to make some reply, when old Nicholas came into the room, and I fancied I could see Mr. Wynkoop stiffen to defend his conduct against inevitable sarcasms.

"Fine doings!" Old Nicholas growled. "The New Englanders had their way, as I expected. I warned you against meddling with treason."

"Treason's a strong word, sir."

"The Association smells of it."

"I cannot think so, sir. The Association is a voluntary agreement not to do certain things; not to import or to export certain goods after a certain date. No law that I know of compels me to import or to export."

"No law requires you to import or to export, very true. But does any law require *me not* to import or export? Certainly no law of the British Parliament or of New York Province obliges me. But suppose I exercise my lawful privilege of importing after the date fixed? What then? Will not your Association compel me not to import, or try to do so? Are not your committees pledged to inspect the customs, to seize my goods, and to sell them at public auction for the benefit of the starving mechanics of Boston? I tell you your Association erects a government unknown to the law; a government which aims to exert compulsion on all citizens. When I am given a coat of tar for violating the Association, will you still say it is a *voluntary* Association?"

"I think little compulsion will be necessary," Mr. Wynkoop replied. "The continent is united as never before; and when the British people realize that, and when British merchants find markets wanting, ministers will be made to see reason."

"You signed the Association, I hear."

"I did, sir. I was opposed to it as Mr. Jay was, but when it was finally carried we both signed it. Once adopted as expressing the policy of Congress, it seemed useless to advertise our divisions, and so weaken the effect of the measures taken. Congress has decided. The important thing now is not what policy Congress should have adopted; the important thing now is for all to unite in support of the policy which it has in fact adopted. If the Colonies present a united front to Britain, as they will do, Britain must yield."

"My advice," old Nicholas said as we went into dinner, "is to drop it. And don't say I didn't warn you."

Over our after dinner wine the matter was gone into at greater length. I said but little, no more than to throw in a remark now and then to keep the argument alive; for I felt that the opposition of old Nicholas would do more to keep Mr. Wynkoop in the right frame of mind than anything I could say. Be that as it may, I left the house well satisfied; for

whether it was the dinner, or the wine, or the truculent arguments of old Nicholas, or all of these combined, I felt sure that the total effect of the evening had been to confirm Mr. Wynkoop in the conviction that the Association was a wise measure, well calculated to bring Britain to terms.

As Mr. Wynkoop had anticipated, little compulsion was necessary to secure the observance of the Association; the threat of confiscation, on the authority of the Committee of 60, of which Mr. Wynkoop was a member, was quite sufficient, save in the case of certain obstinate but negligible traders. And at first it seemed to many that the measures taken would produce the desired effect, for in February Lord North introduced his famous Resolution on Conciliation. I thought the Resolution signified little or nothing, and when in April the news came from Lexington I was not much surprised. It meant war to a certainty, and my first thought was to learn what Mr. Wynkoop would make of it. Curiously enough, with that faculty he had for moulding the world close to the heart's desire, Mr. Wynkoop found some satisfaction in this untoward event. War with Great Britain — no, he would not pronounce the word prematurely. He spoke of the Lexington affair as a repetition of the Boston Massacre, seemingly more serious only because America was now prepared to defend its liberties with arms in its hands. I was delighted that he could take it so; for it convinced me that we might still carry him along with us. The Assembly of New York was too lukewarm to be depended on, half the members or more being frankly Tory, so that we found it convenient to organize a Provincial Congress, composed of delegates elected under the supervision of the Committees, in order to take charge of affairs and keep New York in line with the continent. The most advanced party was already suspicious of Mr. Wynkoop's loyalty; but the moderate men saw the wisdom of winning his support if possible. Mr. Jay and Mr. Alsop were especially keen to have Mr. Wynkoop serve in the Provincial Congress, and they asked me to do what I could to obtain his consent to stand as a candidate.

I did what I could, and I flatter myself that my representations had some influence with him. Knowing his admiration for Mr. Jay, I put it to him as a thing strongly urged by that gentleman.

"Mr. Jay thinks it the more necessary," I said to Mr. Wynkoop, "for men of your sound and moderate views to serve, since the Mechanics are every day gaining headway, and at the same time many men of standing are withdrawing altogether. There is a twofold danger to meet; we must keep the province loyal to the cause, and we must prevent the levelling ideas of the New Englanders from gaining the ascendancy here. If men of your standing refuse to direct the affairs of the colony in these crucial times we shall surely succumb to one or the other of these evils."

"I understand that very well," Mr. Wynkoop replied, "but the decision is not, as you know, an easy one for me."

"Your difficulties are appreciated, and by no one more than by Mr. Jay and all his friends. But it is precisely for that reason, as they point out, that we need your support. Old Nicholas is known to be Tory, and it is much commented on that the Van Schoickendinck Interest is largely lukewarm if not actually hostile. The family Interest is a powerful one, and if you are cordially with us it will do much to bring over many who are hesi-

tating. Your responsibility is the greater, as Mr. Jay rightly says, because of the fact that you will carry with you, one way or another, a great number."

"It is very flattering of Mr. Jay to say so."

Mr. Wynkoop had a great respect for Mr. Jay's judgment — had always had. He consented to stand, and was elected. Throughout the summer of 1775 he attended the sessions of the Provincial Congress faithfully, giving his support to those who were endeavoring to hold the province to a sane middle course — enforcing the Association; raising a militia for defense; keeping the door carefully open for conciliation. Old Nicholas charged him with being too much led about by Mr. Jay. Mr. Wynkoop naturally replied that the notion was ridiculous. What kept him to the mark I feel sure was the feeling that his views and his conduct had been hitherto justified by events, and were now justified by Lord North's Resolution on Conciliation. On this he placed all his hopes. Unacceptable Lord North's Resolution was, he told me on one occasion; but he regretted that the Congress at Philadelphia had seen fit to pronounce it "unseasonable and insidious." When bargains are to be struck, Mr. Wynkoop said, politicians do not offer everything at the first approach. The Resolution proved, he thought, that Lord North was preparing to retreat, as gracefully as possible no doubt. Meantime the policy adopted by the Philadelphia Congress Mr. Wynkoop thought eminently satisfactory; the Resolution on Taking up Arms was admirably phrased to convince Britain that America would defend her rights; the Petition to the King admirably phrased to prove her loyalty. Throughout the summer and autumn Mr. Wynkoop therefore held the

same language to men of extreme views
– to the over timid and to the over zealous: the Petition's the thing, he said; it
will surely effect the end desired.

Hope delayed makes the heart sick, it
has been said. But I think this was not
the effect on Mr. Wynkoop. On the contrary, I am sure that for four months he
found peace of mind by looking forward
to the happy day when the king would
graciously make concessions. I had little
expectation of any concessions, and it
was no great shock to me when the news
arrived in November that the king had
not even deigned to receive the Petition,
much less to answer it. But I knew it
would be a heavy blow to Mr. Wynkoop;
and when the British government, placing an embargo on American trade, proclaimed America to be in a state of rebellion, it is not too much to say that
Mr. Wynkoop's little world of opinion
and conduct, held together by recollection of the past and hope for the future,
was completely shattered. For a month
I saw him scarcely at all. He rarely went
abroad, even to attend the Provincial
Congress. He must have sat at home in
seclusion, endeavoring to adjust his
thought to the grim reality, gathering
together as best he could the scattered
fragments of a broken faith.

During the winter of '76 I saw him
more frequently. We often discussed the
situation at length. The time for discussion, for discussion of the past that is,
seemed to me to be over. But Mr. Wynkoop was seemingly more interested in
discussing what had happened than in
discussing what ought now to be done.
At first this puzzled me; but I soon
found the explanation, which was that
he knew very well what had to be done;
or at least what he had to do, and was
only engaged in convincing himself that

it had been from the first inevitable, that
the situation that now confronted him
was not of his making. His one aim from
the first, he said, and he said it many
times, was to prevent the calamity now
impending. I know not how many times
he reviewed his past conduct. Short of
tamely submitting to the domination of
Parliament, he was forever asking, what
other course could America have followed but the one she had followed?
What other course could he have followed? If America had appealed, not to
force but to reason, was this not due to
the efforts of men of substance and standing, men of Mr. Wynkoop's class? If Mr.
Wynkoop and all his kind had washed
their hands of the affair, would not the
populace and their hot headed leaders
long since have rushed America into violence, and so have given Britain's measures the very justification which they
now lacked?

In all this I quite agreed with Mr.
Wynkoop. I assured him that his conduct had always been that of a wise and
prudent man, and that if events had dis-
appointed the expectations of prudent
men, the fault was clearly not his.
Responsibility lay with the British government, with those mad or unscrupulous
ministers who, wittingly or unwittingly,
were betraying the nation by doing the
will of a stubborn king. Mr. Wynkoop
found consolation in the thought that
since ministers had appealed to the
sword, the decision must be by the sword.
Fight or submit, they had said. The alternative was not of America's choosing, nor
of Mr. Wynkoop's choosing. Could
America submit now? Could Mr. Wynkoop submit now? Whatever he might
have done a year ago, two years ago,
could be now tamely submit, bowing the
head like a scared school boy, renounc-

ing the convictions of a lifetime, advising the friends with whom he had been associated on committees and congresses to eat their words, to cry out for mercy, saying that they did not mean what they said, saying that it was only a game they were playing. "I have made commitments," Mr. Wynkoop often said to me. "I have given hostages." This was true, and this I think was the consideration of greatest weight with him; he could not deny his words and renounce his friends without losing his self respect.

War with Great Britain! Mr. Wynkoop was forced to pronounce the word at last. But independence! That was the hardest word of all. Yet the word was in the air, passing from mouth to mouth behind closed doors and in the open streets. I had long since accustomed myself to the idea, but Mr. Wynkoop hated the thought of it, said he had never desired it, did not now desire it —"unless," he admitted as a kind of after thought, "the Britain I have always been loyal to proves an illusion." It was this notion, I think, that enabled Mr. Wynkoop to reconcile himself to the policy of separation. The Britain of his dreams was an illusion. The Britain he had known did not exist. In those days we were all reading the fiery papers of Mr. Paine entitled *Common Sense*. I know that Mr. Wynkoop read them, and I fancy that they helped him to see Britain in her true colors.

"I like neither the impudence of the man's manner nor the uncompromising harshness of his matter," Mr. Wynkoop once said to me. "Yet it seems that events give only too much foundation for his assertion that we have deluded ourselves in proclaiming the advantages of the connection with Britain. I can't agree with him that the loyal and respectful tone of our pamphlets and petitions is no more than mawkish sentiment; but I do

wonder if the alleged benefits of the union with Britain are but figments of the imagination. It is hard to think so. And yet what now are those benefits? We must surely ask that."

Thus in the long winter of '76 Mr. Wynkoop repaired the illusions by which he lived, reconciling himself to the inevitable step. At this time he saw little of Mr. Van Schoickendinck — it was too painful for both of them, I dare say. At least their last conversation I know (it was by Jeremiah's express invitation that I was present) was a trying one. It was on the 30th of May that we found old Nicholas in the hall of his house, standing, leaning on his cane, evidently much moved.

"I asked you to come," old Nicholas said after greeting us a little stiffly, "because I must know what you purpose to do. General Howe is about to take New York. The Philadelphia Congress is about to declare a separation from Great Britain. The so-called Provincial Congress of New York will hesitate, but it will probably support the measure. Am I to understand that you will burn your bridges and side with the rebels?"

With great seriousness and gravity, Mr. Wynkoop replied:

"I wish you to believe, sir, that I have given the matter every consideration in my power; and it seems to me that I can't do other than go with America. America is my country, and yours too, sir."

"America *is* my country." The voice of old Nicholas was shrill. "I have no great love for Britishers, as you know. Damn them all, I say! But I am too old to meddle with treason. Especially when it can't come to any good. Either we shall be crushed, in which case our last state will be worse than our first; or we shall succeed, in which case we shall be ruled by the mob. Which is better, God knows.

What I can't see is why you have allowed the fanatics to run away with the cart. Fight if you must, but why close the door to reconciliation by declaring an independency?"

"We can't fight without it, sir. That's the whole truth of the matter. I was much against it, and so were most. But the necessity is clear. First we refused to trade, hoping that Britain would make terms as she had formerly done. Instead of making terms Britain closed our ports and prepared to make war. To fight we must have supplies and munitions. We must have money. We can get none of these things without reviving trade; and to revive trade we must have allies, we must have the support of France. But will France aid us so long as we profess our loyalty to Britain? France will give money and troops to disrupt the British empire, but none to consolidate it. The act of separation will be the price of a French alliance."

"Am I to understand that the act of separation is not to be seriously made, except to buy French assistance? That you will let France go by the board as soon as Britain is willing to negotiate?"

Mr. Wynkoop did not at once reply. After a moment he said,

"No, I would not say that, sir. The act of separation is intended for Britain's benefit too. It will make it plain that we mean what we say — that we mean to defend our liberties to the last ditch if necessary. Yet I hope, and believe, in spite of all, that it will not come to that."

For a long moment old Nicholas stood stiff and silent. Suddenly extending his hand, but turning his face away, he said,

"Well, good bye. Our ways part then."

"Don't say that, sir."

"I must say it. I must remain as I began — a loyal British subject. You have ceased to be one. I am sorry to have seen this day. But I must submit to necessity, and you must too."

Slowly old Nicholas ascended the stairs, tapping each tread with his cane. Half way up, he cried out, as if in anger,

"Good bye, I say!"

"God keep you, sir," was all Mr. Wynkoop could find to reply.

Mr. Wynkoop afterwards told me that he spent a sleepless night in his half-abandoned house. In anticipation of General Howe's arrival he had already begun to move his effects out of the city, into Westchester County, near White Plains, where the Provincial Congress was adjourned to meet on July 2. With the business of settling his personal affairs to the best advantage he was so fully occupied that he did not attend the Congress on the opening days. But on the afternoon of the 9th of July he took his place, a little late. Slipping quietly into a vacant chair just in front of me, he was handed a copy of "A Declaration by the Representatives of the United States of America, in Congress Assembled." The chairman of a committee, appointed to report on the validity of the reasons given for separation from Great Britain, was reading the document. We listened to the felicitous and now familiar phrases — "hold these truths to be self-evident"—"just powers from the consent of the governed"—"right of the people to alter or abolish it"—

"Who are the people?" I heard Mr. Wynkoop murmur to his neighbor.

His neighbor, not hearing or not understanding him, whispered behind his hand,

"This is not an easy time for you, I dare say. Mr. Van Schoickendinck can't be induced to join us." The last a statement rather than a question.

"No," Mr. Wynkoop said. "He will go Tory. He will not oppose us. His sympathies are with us really, I think. He is thoroughly American, with no great love for Britain. But he is old — he will go Tory."

"The Declaration will carry, I think."

"Yes."

"It seems well phrased. Jefferson's pen, I understand."

Presently the chairman, having finished the reading of the Declaration, read the report of the committee. "While we lament the cruel necessity which has made that measure unavoidable, we approve the same, and will, at the risk of our lives and fortunes, join with the other colonies in supporting it."

The report of the committee was carried, unanimously, a bare majority being present.

Whereupon a member begged leave, before proceeding to other routine business, to make a few remarks. Permission being granted, the member spoke of the decisive step which had just been taken; of the solemn crisis which confronted all America; of the duty of meeting that crisis with high courage, with the indomitable perseverance of freemen fighting for their liberties. "The time for discussion is over," he said. "The time for action has come. Once thoroughly united, we cannot fail, and if we triumph, as we shall, a grateful posterity will recall these days, and do honor to the patriotic men whose conduct was inspired by the spirit of freedom. God grant we may so act that the spirit of freedom will ever be synonymous with the spirit of '76!"

In the perfunctory applause which greeted these remarks, Mr. Wynkoop joined, as heartily I think, as . . .

Here, most unfortunately, the manuscript ends. What the conclusion of the story may have been, if indeed it ever was concluded, will probably never be known.

John C. Miller:

THE DECLARATION OF INDEPENDENCE

WITH the publication of *Common Sense* in January 1776, Tom Paine broke the ice that was slowly congealing the revolutionary movement. He called boldly for a declaration of independence on the ground that the events of the nineteenth of April, 1775, had put an end to all possibility of permanent reconciliation. By its own act, he argued, Britain had become an open enemy and no American could hereafter "love, honor, and faithfully serve the power that hath carried fire and sword into the land." But there was good even in the evil wrought by British imperialists: it had hastened the dissolution of a union between England and America which Paine regarded as "repugnant to reason, to the universal order of things; to all examples from former ages."[1] Nature herself had de-

[1] *Selections from the Works of Thomas Paine,* edited by A. W. Peach, New York, 1928, 23.

From *Origins of the American Revolution* by John C. Miller, copyright 1943 by John C. Miller. Reprinted by permission of Little, Brown and Company.

creed the separation; and Paine urged Americans, instead of whining after the British connection, to accept their destiny by thundering across the Atlantic a declaration of independence that would shake the throne itself.

Common Sense was epochal not merely because it placed the issue of independence for the first time squarely before the American people. It marked as well the first vigorous attack upon the King — the strongest bond of union yet remaining in the British Empire — and likewise the first appeal for an American Republic. One of Paine's principal arguments for independence was that the King was a "hardened, sullen-tempered Pharaoh," "the Royal Brute of Great Britain" whose determination to extirpate liberty throughout his dominions made it impossible for free Americans to remain within the empire.[2] He opened the eyes of thousands of Americans to the realities of British politics. He demolished in *Common Sense* the fiction that there was a distinction between the King and the Ministry and between the King and Parliament. The King, he declared, had joined forces with Parliament in order to strip Americans of their freedom; far from being in the clutches of wicked ministers, George had made the Ministry his cat's-paw. By means of pensions and places, the King had made himself master of the state: "Wherefore, tho' we have been wise enough to shut and lock a door against absolute Monarchy, we at the same time have been foolish enough to put the Crown in possession of the key."[3] As a result, the Crown had "engrossed the Commons" and had so effectively destroyed the only parts of the British Constitution worth preserving that Eng-

land was hardly better than a European despotism.

After the publication of *Common Sense,* the hottest blasts of patriot propaganda were directed against the King, and the full iniquity of George III was exposed to Americans who had only recently revered him as the best of kings. He was denounced as the evil genius of the British Empire: every oppression perpetrated by the British government during his reign was suddenly laid at his door. The kindest word that could be said for George was that he was either a fool or a villain — "In either case," it was added, "he is no good King."[4] After *Common Sense,* the doctrine of ministerial responsibility — by which Americans had repeatedly saved the King's face — was discredited: the "Royal criminal," it was said, could no longer hide behind the skirts of his ministers; he was revealed as the true malefactor and "the influence of bad Ministers is no better apology for these measures, than the influence of bad company is for a murderer, who expiates his crimes under a gallows."[5] He was denounced as "our damn'd Tyrant of St. James's — a full blooded Nero," and it was said that nurses would soon frighten children into obedience by telling them that "the King will fetch 'em away."[6]

Thus George III became the incarnation of evil as previously he had been the embodiment of every virtue. Both views were distortions: Americans never had a proper perspective of their hapless sovereign. He was neither an innocent young man misled by wicked ministers nor a cunning tyrant determined to

2 *Ibid.,* 25.

3 *Ibid.,* 8.

4 *New York Journal or General Advertiser,* January 25, 1776.

5 *American Archives,* Fourth Series, V, 129, 181.

6 *Pennsylvania Evening Post,* June 13, 1776. *The Lee Papers,* I, 214.

stamp out every vestige of liberty in the empire. George III belongs neither among the angels nor among the devils: he was rather the incarnation of the average rural Englishman of his day. The most just criticism that may be made of his policy is that it never rose above the level of the country gentlemen of England. If his leadership was not inspired, it was at least founded upon the solid rock of British prejudice. Instead of resisting public opinion, he permitted himself to be carried along by it. But in this critical period of the British Empire what was needed was not a spokesman of the lesser squirearchy but the leadership of a man of imperial vision who rose above the prejudices that hemmed in the mind of the majority of Englishmen. Had George III possessed such vision, he might have saved the British Empire. He lost the empire not so much because he was a tyrant as because his outlook was that of the great majority of his subjects: narrow, insular, and contemptuous of "colonists."

Paine did more than smash the oversized statue of George III: he ripped up monarchy root and branch by pronouncing it to be a form of government condemned by the Almighty and by right reason. He traced the origin of kings to robber barons who owed their rise to "savage manners or pre-eminence in subtility"; and the rule of men who excelled in craft or guile was not, Paine contended, fit for free Americans.[7] Before Common Sense, Americans had professed to reverence the British Constitution and had declared that they were defending their own liberties and the rights of the King against the usurpations of Parliament. But Paine's attack upon the principle of monarchism struck at the very foundations of the British Constitution and largely destroyed its sanctity in the eyes of Americans. Its abuses and shortcomings were now laid bare in order to persuade the colonists of the necessity of independence; the beauties which Americans had once beheld in it withered under the blasts of Tom Paine and his fellow propagandists. The British Constitution, it was now said, "gives to some to wallow in luxury to destroy themselves, and forces the greater part to live in poverty. And hence innumerable robberies and executions, which have scarce made their appearance in the Colonies, except imported from the British Constitution." It was nothing more than an instrument to make easier the exploitation of the poor by the rich; and it made legislators of men who, "brought up in luxury, pride and ambition," knew nothing of law and right but were expert in tyrannizing over their fellow men.[8]. . .

The success of Common Sense showed the radicals that they might safely rush in where Tom Paine had not feared to tread. They discovered that they could write the word "independence" without a quaver and that a large number of Americans could bear to look upon it. Thus fortified, they took up their pens and carried on Paine's work of cramming "wholesome truths . . . down the throats of squeamish mortals" and opening American eyes to the unpleasant reality that they must choose between slavery and independence. They were not content, however, to present independence merely as a painful necessity; on the contrary, they painted rosy pictures of the glorious future that awaited Americans after they had cast off the dead hand of Britain. The Tories emphasized the safety and security of remaining with the Brit-

---

[7] Selections from the Works of Thomas Paine, 13.

[8] American Archives, Fourth Series, V, 854.

ish Empire and the advantage of doing business within its vast protected market, but the radicals pictured the wealth that awaited Americans when the markets of the world were open to them. Free trade, it was asserted, would enable Americans to attain "a state of eminence and glory, and become the envy and admiration of mankind"; when no longer plundered by the British House of Commons and hampered by British commercial laws, they would find the riches of the world at their feet. By declaring their independence, Americans could resume the westward advance over the Alleghanies — barred now by the Proclamation of 1763 and the Quebec Act — and take possession of lands which would keep them "free from slavery and taxation to all generations." It would keep America out of Europe's wars: no longer, said Franklin, would Englishmen be able to "drag us after them in all the plundering Wars, which their desperate Circumstances, Injustices, and Rapacity, may prompt them to undertake." It would, in short, enable America to achieve her destiny of a "Great Empire" and thereby fulfill the will of God and Nature. The American continent which teemed "with patriots, heroes, and legislators, who are impatient to burst forth into light and importance," would attain its true greatness — to the delight of all "the inhabitants of Heaven" who longed to see "the ark finished, in which all the liberty and true religion of the world are to be deposited."[9]

These glowing prospects of future wealth and grandeur by no means converted all Americans to independence. The Whigs complained that "puling pusillanimous cowards" continued to spread defeatism; and probably a majority of the American people still thought in terms of reconciliation with the mother country and expected Congress to produce a plan of "permanent" union.[10] The Continental Congress was clearly split by the issues raised by *Common Sense:* "We do not treat each other with that decency and respect that was observed heretofore," lamented a member.[11] In January 1776, James Wilson moved that Congress dispel the rumors that it was aiming at separation by publicly denying any intentions of declaring independence. Although the radicals mustered their utmost strength to defeat this proposal, they were unable to do more than win a postponement of discussion. The ideas of John Dickinson, rather than those of Sam Adams, were still in the ascendancy. The disposition of the majority to allow valuable time to slip away while the British government prepared to overwhelm the colonies with military force led Sam Adams to suggest that the confederation be formed by the few resolute colonies that dared defy Great Britain and that the other colonies be left to make peace as they saw fit.

In the spring of 1776, the British government widened the breach between the opponents and advocates of independence by announcing its intention of sending commissioners to the colonies bearing peace overtures. With the murky waters of independence and republicanism rising about their feet, conservatives found in this commission a straw at

9 *American Archives,* Fourth Series, V, 87, 131, 213, 856. *The Writings of Benjamin Franklin,* VI, 312. David Ramsay, *The History of the American Revolution,* I, 439. Jacob Green, *Observations on the Reconciliation of Great Britain and the Colonies,* Philadelphia, 1776, 25–26. *The Lee Papers,* I, 260, 325. *Virginia Gazette* (Purdie), March 29, 1776.

10 *Pennsylvania Evening Post,* February 3, 1776.

11 *Letters of Members of the Continental Congress,* I, 401.

which to clutch. They would have been disagreeably surprised had they known how reluctantly the British government had agreed to make this eleventh-hour attempt at reconciliation. It was only with the greatest difficulty that George III was persuaded to give his consent. "I am not so fond of the sending Commissioners to examine into the disputes," he said; "this looks so like the Mother Country being more affraid of the continuance of the dispute than the Colonies and I cannot think it likely to make them reasonable; I do not want to drive them to despair but to Submission, which nothing but feeling the inconvenience of their situation can bring their pride to submit to." Although "a thorough friend to holding out the Olive Branch," George wished first to administer some wholesome and, as he suspected, long-overdue chastisement.[12] Unhappily for George's plans, the Brothers Howe — the admiral and the general, in whose ability to crush the revolt great confidence was placed — declined to undertake the subjugation of the colonies unless they were given authority to enter into peace negotiations. George yielded grudgingly to their ambition of carrying both the sword and the olive branch. They were designated as peace commissioners but, as Americans later learned, they were empowered only to accept the submission of the colonies, not to negotiate a settlement which would guarantee American liberties within the empire.

But until this fact was known, conservatives continued to urge that the question of independence be shelved until after the terms of the commission had been received by Congress. They argued so plausibly for delay that the radicals began to regard the commission-

ers as more dangerous to the cause of independence than the British army: they were "the wooden horse which is to take those by stratagem whom twelve years of hostility could not reduce."[13] The radicals declared that while the British government sought to confuse and disunite Americans, whole armies were being equipped "to butcher us with the utmost expedition." Those who advocated waiting for the peace terms found themselves exposed to the radicals' deadliest propaganda. They were called "timid, irresolute and double faced," traitors who opened their "mouths wide, and bawled stoutly against every vigorous measure" because they expected the commissioners' pockets to be "well lined with English guineas, patents for places, pensions and titles in abundance." In exchange for British gold, these turncoats were declared to be ready to open negotiations with "men who spill your blood with as little ceremony and reluctance, as a butcher would that of an ox."[14]

Had the British government pursued consistently this policy of dividing and bewildering Americans by holding out the prospect of reconciliation, the Declaration of Independence might have been postponed and the rebellion crushed. But the mother country, while holding an olive branch in one hand, brandished a sword in the other. *Common Sense* was without doubt a potent force for independence, but its effect, a patriot observed, was "trifling compared with the effects of the folly, insanity and villainy

12 *The Correspondence of King George the Third*, III, 156, 175.

13 William B. Reed, *The Life and Correspondence of Joseph Reed*, Philadelphia, 1847, I, 173.

14 *Pennsylvania Evening Post*, March 2, 1776. *Virginia Gazette* (Purdie), April 19, 1776. *Letters of Members of the Continental Congress*, I, 433, 502. *American Archives*, Fourth Series, V, 89, 433. James Read to Edward Shippen, May 18, 1776, Shippen MSS., Historical Society of Pennsylvania.

of the King and his Ministers."[15] The New England fisheries were closed; the shipment of war supplies to the colonies was forbidden; colonial trade was prohibited; and on December 22, 1775, Parliament withdrew British protection and directed the seizure and confiscation of American ships at sea. As Edmund Burke said, this legislation made England appear "like a porcupine, armed all over with acts of parliament, oppressive to trade and America." Certainly these measures helped the radicals to wean Americans from dependence upon the mother country. John Adams declared that the British government, by removing its protection from the colonies, had cast them out of the empire and made them independent "in spite of our supplications and entreaties."[16] He contended that the colonies had owed obedience to the mother country only because it protected them; now that they were no longer protected, they were not obliged to obey. The radicals insisted that to declare independence was merely to proclaim to the world the true situation in which the colonies found themselves by the act of Great Britain; the British government had itself "dissevered the dangerous tie: Execrated will he be by the latest posterity who again joins the fatal cord!"[17]

Of all the acts of "transcendent folly and wickedness" perpetrated by the British Ministry, none did more to convince Americans of the necessity of an immediate declaration of independence than the hiring of foreign mercenaries to help suppress the rebellion in the colonies. Reports were heard in the colonies early in 1776 that the British government was scouring Europe for mercenaries to employ against Americans; it was remarked that twenty thousand Russian mercenaries would be "charming visitors at New York and civilize that part of America wonderfully."[18] Unable to secure the services of these apostles of sweetness and light because of the refusal of Catherine the Great to permit her subjects to fight on Britain's side, the government turned to the German states for manpower, and thereby revealed to the alarmed colonists that the mother country was an "old stern, encroaching stepdame" who tried to collect all the neighborhood bullies to beat up her children. If Britain called upon Europe to help in the subjugation of the colonies, America must clearly do likewise: France must be made a counterweight to the German states and redress the balance of power upon the American continent. More than any other act of the British government, the hiring of mercenaries opened the eyes of Americans to their own peril and to the impossibility of reconciliation. The patriots declared that it was "the *finishing stroke* to dependence. The man who now talks of reconciliation and reunion, ought to be pelted with stones, by the children, when he walks the streets, as a town fool."[19] The news that Britain had called upon the German princes for aid "wrought wonders" in Philadelphia: "Conversions have been more rapid than ever under Mr. Whitefield" (the evangelist), observed a Philadelphian. Even John Dickinson's faith in the essential goodness of the mother country was momentarily shaken and he

15 *Pennsylvania Evening Post*, March 7, 1776.

16 *Letters of Members of the Continental Congress*, I, 406. *Parliamentary History*, XVIII, 769.

17 *Letters of R. H. Lee*, I, 177. *Pennsylvania Evening Post*, February 3, 1776.

18 Keith Feiling, *The Second Tory Paper*, London, 1938.

19 David Ramsay, *The History of the American Revolution*, I, 427. *Pennsylvania Evening Post*, March 2, 1776.

was heard to say that he saw no alternative but independence or slavery.[20]

While the British government was thus laying its hand rudely upon the "delicate Chinese vase," the friends of the empire in the colonies were losing their struggle to preserve British sovereignty. In Virginia, many members of the tidewater aristocracy arrayed themselves on the side of reconciliation. From the beginning of the dispute with Great Britain, the great planters had been alarmed by the growing power of the Western radicals allied with younger sons of the lowland families and disaffected elements of the East. The aristocracy had carried on the struggle for colonial rights for generations; but they had never sought complete independence of Great Britain nor had they contemplated an internal revolution which would snatch the reins of authority from their own hands, and even in 1776 they refused to admit that the conflict with Great Britain could be resolved only by American independence. These conservatives, said Charles Lee, were "Namby Pambys" whose "little blood has been suck'd out by musketoes"; and when they were confronted with the necessity of declaring independence, "stammer'd nonsense that wou'd have disgraced the lips of an old Midwife drunk with bohea-Tea and gin."[21] As long as the connection with Great Britain was retained, there remained hope that they would be returned to power with the aid of the royal governor; independence meant, on the other hand, the triumph of radicalism and the rule of a new class of men. Thus the fate of the old families of Virginia seemed to depend upon the continuation of the British connection; once that was severed, Pendletons, Robinsons, Randolphs, Nicholases, Blairs, and Tylers might find their estates and privileges at the mercy of their enemies.[22]

The influence of these Virginia conservatives was undermined by the acts of their friends almost as much as by their foes. Early in 1775, Lord Dunmore, the royal governor of Virgina, removed the powder stored in Williamsburg, and put it aboard a British ship. The patriots demanded its return but Dunmore refused to be moved by threats, despite the fact that he could muster only about forty men, most of them sailors, in defense of the capital. Dunmore's weakness was well known to the patriots; and Patrick Henry had little difficulty in rousing the country and encircling Williamsburg with armed men to prevent the escape of the royal governor to the man-of-war lying at York. Had Dunmore enjoyed the support of an army, fighting might have broken out in Virginia at almost the same time that the New England farmers fell upon the British at Lexington; but even bloodshed could hardly have reacted more disastrously upon the conservative cause than did Dunmore's next move. In his desperation, the royal governor summoned the Negro slaves to his standard by promising them emancipation. To Virginians, this was nothing less than a call for race war. Immediately the patriots proclaimed themselves the champions of white supremacy against the British government, which, they declared, was at the bottom of this "hellish plot." With the blessing of the British Ministry, Dunmore was said to be intriguing with the Indians to

[20] Edward Shippen to Jasper Yeates, January 19, 1776, Shippen MSS., Historical Society of Pennsylvania.

[21] Charles Lee to R. H. Lee, April 5, 1776, Lee MSS., American Philosophical Society. *The Lee Papers*, II, 3.

[22] C. H. Ambler, *Sectionalism in Virginia*, Chicago, 1910, 5, 22, 27.

attack the frontiers and holding nightly meetings with the Negroes "for the glorious purpose of enticing them to cut their masters' throats while they are asleep."[23] The report quickly spread over the Southern colonies that British secret agents were arming slaves and Indians; and it was rumored that the King had promised that every Negro who murdered his master would receive the plantation and all the property which had belonged to his owner. The result was that panic swept the South; troublemakers among the slaves were rounded up and patrols went through the town streets every night to enforce the strict curfew that had been clamped down on the Negroes. However groundless this alarm may have been, it weakened Southerners' loyalty to the British government, which now stood arraigned as the upholder of emancipation and black domination of the South. No government thus indicted could long retain the support of Southerners. "Hell," exclaimed a Southern patriot, "would be ashamed of such mean and more than brutal attempts to destroy us, and the devil would blush at the impudence of the man who would have the effrontery to recommend a re-union with so barbarous a government."[24]

Despite the blunders of the British government and the royal governors, the Carolina and Georgia patriots encountered a formidable obstacle to the revolutionary cause in the Western settlers and frontiersmen. The memory of the Regulators' War was still fresh and nothing had been done to remove the grievances which had led the backwoodsmen to take up arms in 1770. They feared that in joining the East against the British government they would find themselves duped by "gentlemen of fortune and ambition on the sea coast." The Southern frontier, like Nova Scotia and the West Indies, was too exposed to Indian incursions and had not yet attained sufficient self-confidence to embark upon revolution. Without British protection, the outlying settlements seemed likely to be at the mercy of the Indians. As late as March, 1774, the Georgia Assembly appealed to the Crown to dispatch more troops for the defense of the frontier. Moreover, the quietist sects — largely German in origin — abounded in the Southern back country. These German sectarians shared the Quakers' scruples regarding war; and to these religious convictions they joined a prudent apprehension of being stripped of their lands if they joined the losing side against the King. The exemption of rice from the Association was also a sore point to the Western settlers: with considerable justice, they charged that they were being asked to bear all the sacrifices of the economic struggle with Great Britain while the lowland planters enjoyed business as usual.[25]

In contrast to the Germans, the Irish (as the Scotch-Irish were known) on the frontier were hot for rebellion. Indeed, throughout the colonies it was enough for Irishmen that England was the enemy: "in a contest with Englishmen,

---

[23] Lord Dunmore to Lord Dartmouth, May 1, 15, 1775, P.R.O., C.O. 5, 1553, Library of Congress Transcript. *Virginia Gazette* (Purdie), October 27, 1775. *American Archives*, Fourth Series, III, 10. *Newport Mercury*, July 31, 1775. *Journal of a Lady of Quality*, 199–200.

[24] *New York Gazette and Weekly Mercury*, April 1, 1776.

[25] Marjorie Louise Daniel, *The Revolutionary Movement in Georgia*, University of Chicago, 1927, Ph.D. Theses (1935), 3–12. *Essays in Honor of William E. Dodd* edited by Avery Craven, Chicago, 1935, 4. David Ramsay, *History of the Revolution in South Carolina*, 65. *New York Gazette and Weekly Mercury*, April 1, 1776.

Irishmen, like the mettlesome coursers of Phaeton, only require reigning in." When in 1774 the assembly of South Carolina asked the governor to give arms to frontiersmen to defend themselves against the Indians, he refused on the ground that Tories, Crown Officers, and even British regulars might, in the eyes of Irishmen, be regarded as better game than redskins. But, except among these Scotch-Irish, Tory propaganda made alarming headway on the Southern frontier. The Tories declared that the dispute was entirely over tea; and since frontiersmen did not drink tea, they ought not to fight the townspeople's battles. Old-wives tales that their lands had been sold secretly by the Whigs to the Indians, "who were to butcher them all on a fixed day," struck terror among the Germans, who refused to sign the Association or to take any part whatever in resisting the British government.

The Southern Whigs could not remain unconcerned by growing Tory strength in the West: the immense number of slaves, the warlike Indians on the frontier, and the open opposition of many Westerners made it doubtful that South Carolina could long resist attack by a British fleet and army. To combat the Tory propaganda and "enlighten" the Western Germans, the Charleston patriots sent William Henry Drayton to the disaffected region. He had little success, although his oratory left "the Mynheers and their Frows" with "watry Eyes." The impressionable frontiersmen were ready to shed tears for the patriot cause, but they made no move to support it. The royal governor of South Carolina too shed tears, but with better effect: he had, complained the Whigs, "found out a mode of talking over some of our Statesmen: he wheedles, & assures, & reasons, & cries like anything." Recognizing that

"an argument relating to money matters most readily catches a Dutchman's ear," the Whigs refused to allow nonsubscribers to the Association to sell or trade at the Charleston stores; all German wagoners entering Charleston were obliged to carry papers proving that they had signed the Association. When even these measures proved ineffectual, the seaboard Whigs were forced to use violence to crush resistance in the interior.[26]

North Carolina, with its considerable population of Scotch (not Scotch-Irish) settlers and unreconstructed Regulators, offered the best prospects to the British government of armed Tory support. Governor Martin of North Carolina declared in 1775 that, given arms and ammunition, he could raise the royal standard in western North Carolina and hold the region against attack. Early in 1776, a British fleet and army under Clinton appeared off Cape Fear; but it was unable to make a junction with the loyalists. Before British aid could reach them the Tories were overwhelmed at Widow Moore's Creek Bridge — the first important battle between Whigs and Tories in the Revolutionary War. The captured loyalists were imprisoned and their property confiscated but many of the rank and file were fortunate enough to get off with a lecture. "I gave them a full and proper account of every thing concerning the ground of the present war," reported a Whig. "This with three or four gallons of rum, was of infinite service to our cause."[27]

[26] R. W. Gibbes, *Documentary History of the American Revolution,* New York, 1885, 128–129, 135. *The South Carolina Historical and Genealogical Magazine,* 1926, XVIII, 134–135. *North Carolina History Told by Contemporaries,* edited by Hugh Lefler, Chapel Hill, 1934, 111.

[27] *Colonial Records of North Carolina,* IX, 1157, 1167, 1174. *New York Gazette and Weekly Mercury,* April 1, 1776.

Elsewhere, during the War of American Independence, Westerners generally supported the Revolution and furnished expert marksmen who laid low many a British redcoat. In Pennsylvania, the backwoodsmen, largely Scotch-Irish Presbyterians, were eager for the fray; the western part of New England became even more warlike than Boston; and the Green Mountain Boys gave an account of themselves that General Burgoyne, for one, found it difficult to forget.

Meanwhile the conservative bloc in the Continental Congress remained adamant in its opposition to independence. Nevertheless, Congress adopted retaliatory measures against the British which went far toward making independence inevitable. In March 1776, Congress authorized the issuance of letters of marque and reprisal against British shipping; and in April 1776 American ports were opened to the ships of all nations except Great Britain. Moreover, patriot blood was being spilled as fighting against British armies broke out on all fronts. Canada was unsuccessfully invaded by American troops under Montgomery and Arnold; the British were forced to evacuate Boston; and American seaports were laid waste by the British navy. It was clear that the colonies were in a state of undeclared war against Great Britain both on sea and on land; and it was becoming increasingly apparent that the struggle could not be waged successfully until the royal governments which still existed in some of the colonies had been overthrown. On May 10, 1776, therefore, Congress advised the conventions and assemblies throughout America to establish governments whose authority was derived from the people instead of from the King. In the preamble to this resolution (adopted May 15), it was declared to be "necessary that the exercise of every kind of authority under the said crown should be totally suppressed." The radicals rightly believed that this measure destroyed the last formidable obstacle to a declaration of independence; all that remained was the mere formality of proclaiming the true state of the relations that had come to exist between the former colonies and Great Britain.

This would have been more apparent to Americans had they known what was going on behind the doors of Congress. Unknown to the people at large, the secret Committee of Correspondence which had been appointed to handle foreign affairs had already sent out feelers for a French alliance. On December 12, 1775, the committee asked Arthur Lee, then in London, to learn the attitude of foreign powers towards the colonies. In February 1776, there was open discussion of a foreign alliance; and in March the committee dispatched Silas Deane to sound out Vergennes, the French minister.

The radicals were in general agreed upon the necessity of foreign alliances; but they were divided over the question whether foreign alliances or a declaration of independence ought to be made first. Many patriots feared to burn the bridges behind them without having made sure of European aid. Even Patrick Henry advised caution: before declaring independence, he said, the Continental Congress ought to feel carefully "the pulse of France and Spain."[28] On the other hand, Alexander Hamilton and Richard Henry Lee argued that France was certain to support the colonies in their struggle with Great Britain if they declared their independence. France, they pointed out, burned for revenge upon Great Britain; and all Europe was

[28] *The Lee Papers*, II, 1–3.

so weary of British bullying that it wished "the haughty empress of the main reduced to a more humble deportment."[29] Only delay in declaring independence could wreck the prospect of a European coalition against Britain. It might require a year in which to consummate a formal alliance with France and Spain; and during that interval British diplomacy would be given an opportunity to drive a wedge between America and her friends upon the European continent. The age was so corrupt, Richard Henry Lee warned, that European nations disposed of "Men & Countries like live stock on a farm," selling whole populations to the highest bidder. There was danger, therefore, that France and Spain might be induced to assist Great Britain to crush the American revolt in exchange for a promise of partition of the American continent. Thus, while Americans were "most dutifully whining after" the British connection and permitting their fears of independence to tie their hands, they might find that their European allies had agreed with England "to share the plunder of America."[30]

Some conservatives feared foreign alliances even more than they did a declaration of independence. Calling in the aid of foreign powers meant not only the end of all hope of maintaining the empire but the unleashing of the dogs of war upon the mother country and so making reconciliation forever impossible. Great Britain might be defeated and overrun by the Bourbons, thus destroying one of the bulwarks of freedom in the world.[31] If Great Britain were con-

quered, and "sunk in the vast Ocean of her own Misconduct," liberty might be overwhelmed in the New World. "Do ye feel no remorse for the ruin of the British empire, the scourge of tyrants, the protector of nations and our sacred religion?" asked a pamphleteer.[32] An independent America, allied with France and Spain, might fall a victim to the very powers which she had joined and become "subject to the Will of some despotic Prince, and be of less Importance than it was whilst in the Hands of the Savages." The North American continent, without British protection, would become a football of contending European powers and become "another Poland" to be divided by aggressor European states; and "mixing the virtuous cause of these Colonies with the ambitious views of France and Spain" was certain to hasten this disaster. No European despotism, above all none with colonial possessions, could be expected to assist the rise of an independent republic in the Western Hemisphere. The greatest danger to American liberty came not from Great Britain but from the Catholic, despotic powers of Europe into whose arms Americans were about to fling themselves.[33] The radicals answered that France and Spain could be trusted to withdraw from the colonies after independence had been achieved and that if Great Britain met with destruction as a result of the loss of her empire, it was her own fault. "If she is ruined," they declared, "it is because she is ripe for ruin, and God's judgments must come

29 *Boston Evening Post*, February 3, 1776. *The Works of Alexander Hamilton*, I, 169.

30 *Letters of R. H. Lee*, I, 177–178. *Virginia Gazette* (Purdie), March 29, 1776.

31 Thomas Bradbury Chandler, *The Ass; or the Serpent*, Boston, 1768, preface.

32 William Smith, *Plain Truth*, Philadelphia, 1776, 105. Robert Nicholas, *Considerations on the Present State of Virginia*, 1774, 9.

33 *Pennsylvania Gazette*, April 3, 1776. *The Address of the People of Great Britain to the Inhabitants of America*, London, 1775, 6. William Smith, 29–30. Friedrich Kapp, *The Life of John Kalb*, New York, 1884, 55.

upon her; in which case we ought to be disunited."[34] The radicals prevailed and, as is well known, the Declaration of Independence was made before France had formally declared herself in alliance with the United States.

In the final analysis, the question of independence was decided not in the Continental Congress but in the states where the issue was threshed out in popular assemblies and meetings. Both conservatives and radicals in Congress appealed to the people outside to voice their wishes; and the people's answer had much to do with the final decision. It was soon made clear that the militant minority that was rapidly coming to dominate the states through committees and revolutionary conventions had little patience with the irresolution displayed by Congress upon the subject of independence. Congress, indeed, was in danger of finding itself left in the wake of public opinion in some states: "The People are now ahead of you," wrote Joseph Hawley of Massachusetts to Sam Adams, "and the only way to prevent discord and dissension is to strike while the iron is hot. The Peoples blood is too Hot to admit of delays — All will be in confusion if independence is not declared immediately. The Tories take courage and Many Whiggs begin to be chagrined — the Speech in Many parts is what is our Congress about? they are *dozing* or amusing themselves or waiting to have a Treaty with Commissioners which will end in our destruction." Hawley predicted that unless Congress acted swiftly "a Great Mobb" of citizens and soldiers would descend upon Philadelphia to purge Congress and set up a dictator.[35]

Virginians were so fiery in the cause, declared Elbridge Gerry, that if Congress did not want to be anticipated by them in making a declaration of independence, it would have to send some Congressmen to Virginia to throw cold water on these red-hot patriots. New Englanders were heard to say, "We must rebel some time or other, and we had better rebel now than at any time to come; if we put it off for ten or twenty years, and let them go on as they have begun, they will get a strong Party among us, and plague us a great deal more than they can now."[36] Time, in other words, seemed to be on the side of the British government and despotism.

A declaration of independence was believed essential to stamping out the growing Tory menace. Although the Tories had begun to flee in 1775 and America seemed in "a fair way of being disgorged of all those filthy, grovelling vermin," those that remained took courage from the divided counsels of the Whigs.[37] Some of them so far recovered from their terror as to grow saucy toward the patriots and taunted them with the charge that they feared to call down the wrath of Great Britain by declaring independence. Early in 1776, General Charles Lee ordered the Tories on Long Island to swear an oath to take up arms if called upon by Congress. Isaac Sears was dispatched to administer the oaths. He met with considerable opposition, however, and reported that when he "tendered the oath to four of the grate Torries," they swallowed it "as hard as if it was a four pound shot, that they were trying to git

---

[34] Green, 18. Edward Shippen to Jasper Yeates, January 19, 1776, Shippen MSS., Historical Society of Pennsylvania.

[35] Joseph Hawley to Samuel Adams, April 1, 1776, Adams MSS., New York Public Library.

[36] *Old Family Letters,* edited by Alexander Biddle, Philadelphia, 1892, 140. *Letters of Members of the Continental Congress,* I, 438. *The Lee Papers,* I, 380, 426.

[37] *Virginia Gazette* (Purdie), September 22, 1775.

down."[38] Lee was reprimanded by Congress for exceeding his authority and the Tories took new heart, which served to confirm the radicals' opinion that a declaration of independence was the only way of giving "that many headed Monster the Tory Faction" a fatal wound by confiscating the estates of wealthy loyalists. It was observed that the Tories, recognizing this danger, hung their heads at the mention of independence. "I wish," said a New Englander, "it may not be long before some are hung by them."[39]

From a mere handful of "oligarchs" in 1765, the Tories had become a powerful minority that included members of all ranks and classes but was particularly well represented in the Northern colonies by the upper class of merchants, landowners, and lawyers. Not all Tories were aristocrats; nor were all Whigs "Ragamuffins"; yet a large proportion of the gentry north of Mason and Dixon's line were openly Tories or secret sympathizers with the mother country. Among the upper class, Toryism came dangerously near being fashionable. In New York City, for example, of the 102 members of the New York Chamber of Commerce, 54 were Tories, 17 were neutral, and 21 were Whigs. In New Jersey, eight out of twelve members of the Council were Tories, as were many of the wealthy merchants and landowners. When the Tories left Boston, it appeared as though the Harvard alumni were pulling up stakes in a body. In Virginia, on the other hand, the aristocrats were staunchly Whig and the Tories were chiefly the Scotch factors and merchants of Norfolk. And in the Carolinas, Toryism flourished largely in the western counties where frontiersmen took the

side of King and Parliament against the eastern Whigs.[40]

The Tories who were driven into exile were a mere handful in comparison to the multitude of trimmers and timid souls who found discretion wiser than active opposition to the Whigs. These fair-weather Tories were outwardly Whigs until the approach of a British army made the countryside safe for Toryism. New York and Pennsylvania harbored so many hot-and-cold Tories that John Adams declared that "if New England on one side and Virginia on the other had not kept them in awe, they would have joined the British."[41] During the early period of the war, the British government relied upon the American loyalists to do a large part of the fighting; but comparatively few Tories sprang to arms. In general, the Tories preferred to sit on the fence, fearful lest by taking sides they would jeopardize their property. Only the most courageous of the loyalists were open Tories, but even they suffered from their inability to unite in defense of their ideals. The Whigs realized that if they did not stand together they would hang together; the Tories, on the other hand, "saw and shuddered at the gathering storm, but durst not attempt to dispel it, lest it should burst on their own heads." Individual Tories hoped that whatever happened to others, they would escape; not until too late did they see that they would go down together once the Whigs gained the upper hand.[42]

[38] The Lee Papers, I, 359.

[39] Richard Derby, Junior, to Samuel Adams, January 19, 1775, Adams MSS.

[40] Quarterly Journal of the New York State Historical Association, October 1932, XIII, 378.

[41] Works of John Adams, X, 63. Lord Dunmore to Lord Dartmouth, June 25, 1775, P.R.O., C.O. 5, 1535, Library of Congress Transcript. Letters of Captain W. G. Evelyn, edited by G. D. Scull, 51.

[42] Rivington's New York Gazetteer, December 22, 1774. The Correspondence of General Thomas Gage, I, 363.

Many of the upper-class Tories were highly cultured pillars of society who put the eighteenth-century ideal of "order and decency" above the rights of man. Like the later American Federalists, they believed that America ought to be ruled by the wise, the good, and the rich — by which they meant, of course, themselves. They loved England and sought to create islands of English manners and ideals in a vast sea of farmers and frontiersmen. They wished well to America — so well, indeed, that they wanted to transplant English institutions, society, and culture to the New World under the firm conviction that America could attain no greater felicity.

The Tories denied that all the virtue was on the side of the Whigs: "The Politician who stuns you with harangues of his own angelic purity," said Daniel Dulany, now turned Tory, "is as certainly an errant imposter as the woman who unceasingly prates of her own chastity, and is no better than she should be."[43] Despite the Whigs' practice of putting into the mouths of Tories doctrines which made them appear to be supporters of the "villainous System of Revenues & Domination, and the "infernal doctrine of arbitrary power" not many of them wholeheartedly approved of the measures of the British government.[44] Far from being the abettors of British tyranny, the Tories were the first to suffer by it; they deplored Parliament's insistence upon taxing the colonies because they, like the Whigs, were upholders of colonial liberties, and recognized that some middle ground must be found between the absolute authority of Parliament and complete independence. As

Governor Tryon of New York said, "Oceans of Blood may be spilt but in my opinion America will never receive parliamentary taxation. I do not meet with any of the Inhabitants who shew the smallest inclination to draw the Sword in support of that principle."[45]

Up to 1776, there was no unbridgeable gulf between the views of the Whigs and Tories as to the rights and liberties of the colonies in the British Empire. Both professed to aim at reconciliation; and both opposed taxation by Parliament. There was, however, a wide difference between them regarding the methods to be used to defend American liberty and in their attitude towards the mother country. The Tories believed that the colonies ought not to go beyond petitions and remonstrances when contesting British authority; they insisted that nothing was to be gained by spitting in the mother country's face and calling her names which should not be heard outside the kennel. Unlike the radicals, they feared the mother country's military might: "Great Britain," they said, was not "an old, wrinkled, withered, worn-out hag, whom every jackanapes that truants along the streets may insult with impunity," but "a vigorous matron, just approaching a green old age."[46] They looked upon her not as a harsh stepmother but as "a fostering parent" who was sorely tempted by colonial unruliness to apply the birch to her offspring. Nor did the Tories make a practice, as did many of the Whigs, of habitually believing the worst of the British government. They never surrendered their hope that the dispute might be settled by

---

[43] *Correspondence of "First Citizen," Charles Carroll of Carrollton and "Antilon," Daniel Dulany, Junior,* edited by E. S. Riley, Baltimore, 1902, 35.

[44] *Massachusetts Spy,* March 9, 1775.

[45] *Documents relative to the Colonial History of the State of New York,* VIII, 604.

[46] William Eddis, *Letters from America,* 94. Samuel Seabury, *A View of the Controversy Between Great Britain and Her Colonies,* New York, 1774, 32.

peaceful means and that "both countries, supporting and supported by each other, might rise to eminence and glory, and be the admiration of mankind till time shall be no more."[47] To the end, they inveighed against the narrow provincialism of which many Whigs were guilty: "Remember that not this, or any other province is your country, but the whole British empire," they reminded Americans.[48]

With Great Britain clearly preparing to crush the revolt by every means in her power and with the fair prospect of despoiling the Tories beckoning Americans, the appeal to the people demanded by the conservatives in the Continental Congress proved a boomerang to the cause of reconciliation. As John Adams said, "Every Post and every Day rolls in upon Us Independence like a Torrent." One of the principal sources of this demand for independence was the American army, where it was observed as early as 1775 that the soldiers did not pray for the King. This spirit began to take possession of the provincial congresses, county conventions, and town meetings, which hastened to add their voices to the clamor. In April 1776, Judge William Henry Drayton of South Carolina declared that Americans were absolved from all allegiance to the King of Great Britain; and the North Carolina Provincial Congress directed its delegates in the Continental Congress to vote for independence and foreign alliances. But the greatest triumph of the radical cause came on May 15, 1776, when the Virginia Convention unanimously instructed its delegates to cast their vote for independence and the "UNION FLAG of the American states" was raised over the capital at Williamsburg.[49]

The last-ditch opposition to independence came from the Middle colonies, where the people were yet unreconciled to shoving off into uncharted waters. The delegates of these colonies in the Continental Congress delighted in tripping up the radicals; "The Proprietary Colonies do certainly obstruct and perplex the American Machine," lamented Richard Henry Lee as he observed the halting progress towards independence. The "feeble politicks" of these colonies repeatedly threatened to disrupt the American union. When Congress urged the Maryland Council of Safety to seize Governor Eden, the Council refused and roundly declared that Congress was attempting to encroach upon colonial rights and make itself dictator of the continent. For this display of bad temper, President John Hancock of the Continental Congress pointedly snubbed the Maryland delegates, but they continued to toss monkey wrenches into the radicals' machinery. Maryland, observed John Adams, was "so eccentric a Colony — sometimes so hot, sometimes so cold," that he wished "it could exchange Places with Hallifax."[50]

From the moment that independence had loomed upon the horizon, the Middle colonies had desperately attempted to arrest its progress. In November 1775, the New Jersey Assembly appointed a committee to draft a petition to the King, whereupon Congress declared that it was "dangerous to the liberties and welfare of America" if any colony

---

[47] Charles Inglis, *The True Interest of America Impartially Stated*, Philadelphia, 1776, 35.

[48] *Rivington's New York Gazetteer*, November 18, 1773.

[49] *Principles and Acts of the Revolution in America*, edited by H. Niles, 111. *Virginia Gazette* (Purdie), May 17, 1776.

[50] *American Archives*, Fourth Series, V, 983, 1010. *Letters of Members of the Continental Congress*, I, 442, 461.

petitioned separately. Congress put John Dickinson at the head of a committee and dispatched it to New Jersey to persuade the assembly not to break the ranks. Dickinson and his colleagues were able to quash the petition but the New Jersey Legislature shortly thereafter assured Governor Franklin that it knew of "no sentiments of independency that are, by men of consequence, openly avowed." The Pennsylvania Assembly followed up this action by instructing the Pennsylvania delegates in Congress "utterly to reject" any attempt to separate the mother country and colonies. New Jersey followed suit and Maryland imposed much the same restrictions upon her delegates.[51]

To the radicals in the Continental Congress, Pennsylvania proved the worst stumbling block of all. As late as May, 1776, the advocates of reconciliation carried the elections in Philadelphia and the merchants refused to join the planters of Maryland and Virginia in making a contract to supply the Farmers-General of France with tobacco on the ground that it would raise a barrier to peace between the mother country and colonies. The radicals railed at the "damned Aristocracy" and the "perverse drivelling knot of Quakers" whose domination of the province throttled support for the revolutionary cause: Pennsylvania, they said, was showing "the moderation of a Spaniel dog, that grows more fond in proportion to the ill usage he received," and Charles Lee recommended that the members of the Pennsylvania Assembly, as punishment for their "damn'd trick of adjourning and procrastinating," be turned out of the Statehouse and sent to Germantown to make stockings for the

army — an occupation, he remarked, "manly enough for 'em."[52]

With many of the delegates from the Middle colonies striving to dam the flood, Congress yielded slowly to the "torrent of Independence." On June 7, 1776, Richard Henry Lee introduced a resolution as he had been directed by the Virginia Convention, to the effect that the "united Colonies are, and of right ought to be, free and independent States," and that foreign alliances and a plan of confederation ought to be created. Largely because the delegates from Pennsylvania, New Jersey, New York, and Delaware had no authority to enter into this resolution, it was decided to postpone the question of independence until July 1. The Middle colonies, it was expected, would use this interval to put themselves on record in favor of independence or at least to remove the restrictions upon their delegates which prevented them from voting for such a declaration. In Pennsylvania, the radicals found it necessary to carry out a *coup d'état* to put the province in line: a Provincial Conference dispossessed the assembly of its authority and on June 24 declared that the province was ready to join the other colonies in declaring independence. Delaware and New Jersey freed their delegates from the restrictions that had hitherto tied their hands; and the Maryland delegation was likewise empowered to vote for independence. By July 1, 1776, Pennsylvania was the only state a majority of whose delegates opposed independence; but with the struggle going steadily

---

[51] *Ibid.*, I, 460. *Documents relative to the Colonial History of the State of New Jersey*, New Series, X, 690–691.

[52] *The Lee Papers*, I, 143, 227, 476. *Report on the MSS. of Mrs. Stopford-Sackville*, II, 22. *Memoirs of the Historical Society of Pennsylvania*, Philadelphia, 1895, XIV, 281. Alexander Graydon, *Memoirs of a Life chiefly passed in Pennsylvania*, 117. *American Archives*, Fourth Series, V, 800. *Virginia Gazette* (Purdie), March 17, 1775.

against them and a backfire springing up in Pennsylvania itself, Robert Morris and John Dickinson, the old guard of the Pennsylvania delegation, absented themselves from Congress on July 2, 1776, and thereby permitted an almost unanimous vote by the states — although not by the delegates themselves — in favor of independence. Because the vote of a state was determined by a majority of its delegates, evidences of dissent in Congress were not revealed to the people. New York, however, having failed to instruct its delegates, voted neither aye nor nay on July 2. On July 4, when the Declaration of Independence was adopted, New York still declined to vote; and it was not until July 15 that the New Yorkers formally threw in their lot with the rebellious states.

The Declaration of Independence, as drawn up by Thomas Jefferson, was the final proof — if Englishmen needed any further proof — that the doctrines of John Locke could be made to serve the purposes of revolutionists everywhere. Many years later, Jefferson said that the Declaration was intended to be "an expression of the American mind"; "I know only that I turned to neither book nor pamphlet while writing it," he said. "I did not consider it as any part of my charge to invent new ideas altogether, and to offer no sentiment which had ever been expressed before." The American mind of 1776 was saturated with John Locke. The Declaration frequently repeats even the phraseology of the philosopher of the "glorious revolution"; and it applies to the dispute between Great Britain and the colonies his compact theory of government and his insistence upon the right of revolution when the existing government has become destructive of the ends for which all governments are instituted. In the final analysis, the separation of Great Britain and the colonies is justified by the natural rights of man which Locke had emphasized rather than upon the narrower rights of British subjects: the colonists had originally become members of the British Empire by their own free will — they withdrew because the King had invaded the inalienable rights which they retained from the state of nature.

The Declaration of Independence submitted "Facts . . . to a candid world" and was written out of "decent respect to the opinions of mankind." This might be held to imply that the Declaration was written chiefly for foreign consumption and that Jefferson's primary purpose was to lay the cause of the United States before the tribunal of world opinion. The character of the "Facts" contained in it militates against this view. It is the iniquity of the King which is held to be the principal, if not the only cause of America's withdrawal from the empire. Parliamentary tyranny — against which the colonists had inveighed for a decade — is almost entirely forgotten. "The history of the present King of Great Britain is a history of repeated injuries and usurpations, all having in direct object the establishment of an absolute tyranny over these States," Jefferson declared; and under twenty-eight headings the crimes of George III are enumerated. It is clear that Jefferson's purpose in portraying the King as the root of all evil in the empire was to convince the vast numbers of Americans who were still unreconciled to independence that their last hope had failed them. Jefferson saw that the overstuffed figure of George III which the patriots had created with their own hands was the last obstacle to independence. The job that Tom Paine had begun in *Common Sense* Jefferson intended to finish in the Declaration of Independence.

While demolishing the reputation of George III and the monarchial ideal itself, Jefferson gave his countrymen a new goal toward which to strive: a republican system of government in which human rights would take precedence over property and privilege. No one who read the Declaration could fail to see that an experiment in human relations was being made and that the new order which it established was to be chiefly for the benefit of the common man. Equality and liberty — government by the consent of the governed — were the ideals now held up to men. Here, surely, the common man was given something to fight for and, if need be, to die for. The war aims of the Revolution were now complete: the struggle against Great Britain was to be waged for independence; for the liberty of the individual; and for the creation of a society in which men were free and equal.

Independence was proclaimed as the portentous shadow of British military might again fell upon the American states. Although the British army had been forced to evacuate Boston in March 1776, on July 3 — the day before the Declaration of Independence was adopted by the Continental Congress — Sir William Howe, at the head of a formidable force, seized Staten Island and began to prepare to drive the American army from Long Island and New York City. The Declaration had come just in time. In the days ahead that were to try men's souls, only the loftiest ideals and most stirring phrases could sustain Americans in their struggle for freedom.

Claude H. Van Tyne:

AMERICAN versus ENGLISH IDEAS OF THE BRITISH CONSTITUTION

H AD it been possible to please both radical colonist and conservative Englishman with some happy solution of the proper extent and character of local self-government, and had that solution included some mode of permitting each integral part of the empire to enjoy what theory and practice of representation it preferred, harmony might have reigned within the British dominions. But if Parliament was to exercise the supremacy to which it made claim, there still remained between the colonial liberal and the British conservative a differing conception of the extent of Parliament's power over the individual citizen which boded ill for any real restoration of good understanding.

Whenever the colonial orator or pamphleteer failed to sustain his argument against an offensive act of Parliament by appeal to charter rights, or to the rights of Englishmen as found in Magna Charta and the Bill of Rights, he took refuge in natural rights, or in his own conception

From *The Causes of the War of Independence* by Claude H. Van Tyne. Houghton Mifflin Company, 1922. Reprinted by permission.

of the British Constitution. It was this dangerous doctrine, "destructive to all government," which the Lords, in their protest against the repeal of the Stamp Act, declared "has spread itself over all our North American colonies, that the obedience of the subject is not due to the laws and legislature of the realm farther than he, in his private judgment, shall think it conformable to the ideas he has formed of a free constitution."[1] Otis resorted to this doctrine in his attack on "Writs of Assistance." That an act of Parliament had made them legal did not pose him. He declared, "no act of Parliament can establish such a writ"; for "an act against the Constitution is void," the courts must pass it into disuse. He implied that the Constitution as he conceived it contained pledges of protection to the rights of the individual which even Parliament could not gainsay. Those pledges were its bounds "which by God and nature are fixed," he declared in his "Rights of the British Colonies." "Hitherto have they a right to come, and no farther." Some seven years later Samuel Adams, expressing the ideas of the Massachusetts House of Representatives, wrote, "It is the glory of the British Prince and the happiness of all his subjects, that their constitution hath its foundations in the immutable laws of nature, and as the supreme legislature as well as the supreme executive derives its authority from that constitution, it should seem that no laws can be made or executed that are repugnant to any essential law in nature."[2] To Adams's mind this "law

in nature" was his own idea of right and wrong. From the days when young Alcibiades asked Pericles the meaning of the word law, learned men have disagreed as to its exact meaning, but Samuel Adams, always in intimate converse with the Oracle of politics, never allowed the shadow of dubiety to rest upon his assumptions. He was always sure that what seemed wrong to him could not be sanctioned by the British Constitution. In fact, he and other Americans were but imitating Pym and Hampden of the older British revolution, in claiming to be already vested with rights, which in reality they were at that moment endeavoring to achieve.[3] His idea of the limitations of Parliament was the prevailing American view, but Lord Mansfield and conservative Englishmen in general rejected it utterly. The British Constitution, they informed him, was the Magna Charta and Bill of Rights and the common law as the British courts throughout the centuries had left it, but in addition to all these elements it was the changing law of Parliament. Even William Pitt, the greatest defender of the colonists' cause, after holding that he thought them "deprived of a right," added, "but by an authority they ought not to question."[4] He merely confessed his faith in the absolute power of Parliament. "What Parliament doth no power on earth can undo" Blackstone had put it (1758) in his lectures at Oxford.[5]. Any act of Parliament might any day change even the Constitution of England.[6] Such

---

[1] Hansard, Parliamentary History, XVI, 186.

[2] Samuel Adams, Writings, I, 190 (writing to Conway, Secretary of State, who had resigned a month earlier, though the colonists did not know it). John Adams wrote (1762), "an act of Parliament against natural equity . . . would be void." John Adams, Works, II, 139.

[3] McLaughlin, The Courts, the Constitution and Parties, 69, 72.

[4] American Historical Review (April, 1912), 573.

[5] Blackstone, Commentaries (1768 ed.), I, 91, 161.

[6] Perhaps the most striking example of that was the Act of 1911 which destroyed the power of the House of Lords.

an idea seemed preposterous to one who drew his political philosophy from colonial experience and the political writers of the seventeenth century. Of a pamphleteer who inferred that Parliament had a right to tax because it resolved that it had, Samuel Adams wrote, with a sneer, "I shall only say that his reasoning is much like that of a late letter writer from London, whose wonderful performance, if I mistake not, was inserted in all newspapers, who says that 'when an Act of Parliament is once passed, it becomes a part of the Constitution.' "[7] The acceptance in England of the supremacy of Parliament was a political habit only lately acquired, while the colonists, who had really broken their British ties in the seventeenth century, were carrying on old English doctrines still in favor when the "Fathers" left the homeland and first set foot in America.[8] As Governor Hutchinson explained to the English agent of his colony, "Our friends to liberty take advantage of a maxim they find in Lord Coke that an act of Parliament against Magna Charta or the peculiar rights of Englishmen is *ipso facto* void." In a word, they were depending on an obsolete law writer whom the British Constitution had outgrown.

The colonial idea as expressed by Otis and Adams was not new in America, for it will be recalled that, when the Puritan magistrates of Massachusetts Bay were asked (1683) to give up their charter which it was argued they had legally forfeited, the ministers who were consulted said that though according to some corrupt and unrighteous laws they might have done so, yet according to laws of righteousness and equity they had not

done so.[9] These were the laws to which Jonathan Mayhew had appealed when in 1750 he held that the King was limited, not merely by acts of Parliament, "but by eternal laws of truth, wisdom, and equity and the everlasting tables of right reason — tables that cannot be repealed, or thrown down and broken like those of Moses."[10] Indeed, long before any American had appealed to natural law, Sophocles expressed the idea in Antigone's defense of her illegal burial of her brother. She acted, she pleaded, in free obedience to the "unwritten and unchanging laws of heaven — laws that are not of to-day or yesterday but abide for ever, and of their creation knoweth no man." The colonists, however, had not drawn their ideas of natural law directly from antiquity, but from writers on political theory in the time of the Stuarts. Locke had said, "A government is not free to do as it pleases . . . the law of nature stands as an eternal rule to all men, legislators as well as others." We find in the debates in Parliament in the ten years preceding the Revolution, nearly as much use of Locke's philosophy as in America, but in England the fixed traditions, the settled customs, the old environment, the established classes determined to resist change, prevented the practical application of the doctrines; while in America the frontier favored experiment and the seed fell on good ground. Contemporaries of Samuel Adams saw reason to lament the "evil Consequences arising from the Propagation of Mr. Locke's democratical Principles,"[11] but before Locke it had been held by Thomas Edwards that, in spite of past laws and agreements, men of the new age

---

[7] Wells, *Samuel Adams*, I, 59.

[8] McLaughlin, *The Courts, the Constitution and Parties*, 81, 91.

[9] Hutchinson Papers in Mass. Hist. Soc., *Collections* (3d Ser.), I, 80.

[10] Thornton, *The Pulpit of the Revolution*, 95.

[11] Dean Tucker, *Four Letters on Important National Subjects*, 89.

ought to enjoy "their natural and just liberties agreeable to right reason."[12] And these writers of the Stuart period were but elaborating the idea of Melanchthon a century earlier who, in defending natural law, said that he relied on the saying of St. Paul that the law is written in the human heart.[13]

Though colonial political literature in the decade before the Declaration of Independence abounds with appeals to this natural law, it had its exponents also in England. Even Blackstone, after declaring that "if Parliament will positively enact a thing to be done which is unreasonable, I know of no power that can control it," goes on to say that in a conflict between legislation and natural law, the latter must prevail. "This law of nature," he explains, "is of course superior in obligation to any other. It is binding all over the globe in all countries and at all times, no human laws are of any validity, if contrary to this."[14]

Both the prevailing colonial mind and that of the English radicals drew from this idea of natural laws, which put bounds to the power of Parliament, a deduction which was to become a fundamental principle in American constitutional law. John Dickinson, after propounding the question, "Who are a free people?" answered with assurance, "Not those over whom Government is reasonably and equitably exercised, but those,

who live under Government, so constitutionally checked and controlled that proper provision is made against its being otherwise exercised."[15] "There are," wrote Samuel Adams, "fundamental rules of the Constitution, which it is humbly presumed neither the supreme legislature nor the supreme executive can alter. In all free states the Constitution is fixed."[16] Adams here expressed the idea which underlies a written constitution, which can be changed solely by the people and only with great difficulty, and which places definite bounds to the power of the legislative and the executive branch of government. It was an idea which grew naturally out of the colonial experience with written charters. They had been used for generations to seeing their legislatures hedged about by fixed law. Their experience was bolstered by the philosophy of great political thinkers whom they reverenced. Both Adams and Otis were acquainted with Vattel, the latest and most popular of continental writers. Indeed, Otis in his "Rights of the Colonists" quotes from Vattel's "Law of Nature and Nations" wherein he asserts that the authority of the legislature does not extend so far as to change the constitution of the state. "It is from the constitution that these legislators derive their power; how can they change it without destroying the foundation of their own authority?" asks Vattel. "They ought to consider the fundamental laws as sacred," he continues, "for the Constitution of the state ought to be fixed."[17] It was an idea full of

12 Thomas Edwards, *The Third Part of Gangræna*, etc., 16–17.

13 Höffding, *History of Philosophy*, I, 40.

14 Blackstone, *Commentaries* (ed., 1768), I, 41, 91. This seeming contradiction Roscoe Pound (*Yale Law Review*, Dec., 1912, pp. 17–19) explains by the historical fact that although after the Revolution of 1688 the absolute supremacy of Parliament was established, yet in fact the great bulk of English law was traditional (formed in theory under the laws of nature), not made by Parliament.

15 John Dickinson, *Memoirs*, Pa. Hist. Soc., XIV, 356; Macdonald, *Documentary Source Book*, 148.

16 The same idea in the "Circular Letter"; also in Samuel Adams, *Writings*, I, 134, 156, 170, 175, 180, 185, 190, 196; II, 325, 350, 452.

17 James Otis, *Rights of the Colonists*, 109; Samuel Adams, *Writings*, II, 325.

promise to men faced with a threat of absolute rule by a parliament three thousand miles away in which they had no voice. Against a conception that the British Constitution was from day to day what Parliament made it was now set the dictum that every free government is bound by fixed law. If a government is bound to regard the unchanging laws of nature, reasoned the American mind, then it is restrained by fixed law and is a free government, and that was what the colonist insisted the British Government would be if not distorted by such "enemies of liberty" as Lord Mansfield.

Americans were not unaware of their inheritance from English history of traditions of freedom growing from precedent to precedent, from Magna Charta to and beyond the Bill of Rights, until English liberty was second to none in all the world. "Here lies the difference between the British Constitution and other forms of government," wrote John Adams in 1766, "that liberty is its end, its use, its designation, drift and scope, as much as grinding corn is the use of a mill."[18] Samuel Adams, too, had paid his tribute (1750). "There is," he wrote, "no form of civil government . . . appears to me so well calculated to preserve this blessing [of liberty] or to secure to its subjects all the most valuable advantages of civil society, as the English."[19] Otis found the British "the most perfect form of government, that in the present depraved state, human nature is capable of."[20] It was long before Otis or the "brace of Adams" realized that what they loved was not the British Government, but their idea of it.

[18] Lord Acton, *Essays on the French Revolution*, 23.

[19] Wells, *Samuel Adams*, I, 21.

[20] Tudor, *James Otis*, 105.

American thought and English thought had come to the parting of the ways. A section of the Anglo-Saxon world was entering on a new stage of the development of free government. Through the efforts of courageous Englishmen the power of the King to rule in an arbitrary manner (except by corruption) had been destroyed, but it was still possible for Parliament to govern in an arbitrary way, and America was to lead in the struggle to establish, at least in the Anglo-Saxon world, a government of law and not of men, of written basic law and not of men raised by their fellows to a little brief authority. For the moment Americans had outstripped Englishmen in the race for political freedom. The absolutism of Parliament was to Otis and Adams as hateful as the absolutism of the King, but for the ruling class in England there was no such fear. From the days of Charles I, the English political development had been in the direction of absorption of power by Parliament, a tendency to concentrate all power legislative and executive in that body. Once it was elected all sovereignty was vested in it, and the English people, or merely that small part which enjoyed the franchise, was sovereign only during an election. Forms still obscured that concentration of power to such a degree that even so profound a student as Montesquieu thought the English political system was a nicely balanced one with the legislative branch carefully set over against the executive and each checking the other. The omnipotence of Parliament, its power to alter the very Constitution of England through its changing laws, was a fact not fully grasped even by Englishmen. However, there were some forward-looking Englishmen who did see it, and who were demanding reform. One must not miss the important fact that the American

Revolution was politically not merely a clash between England and America, but a civil war, a factional war within the British Empire. It must be noted that not only were there Americans who defended the views of the British official middle-class mind, as typified in Mansfield,[21] and Englishmen who were liberal enough, like Pitt and Burke, to let the colonists have their own way because that was expedient, but other Englishmen who truly looked at the British Constitution as did Americans. Lord Camden, appealing to "that consummate reasoner and politician Mr. Locke, whose principles were drawn from the heart of our constitution," declared "as a lawyer" that the Constitution was against taxing the Americans, intimating that a mere act of Parliament would not change the Constitution and thus make such taxation legal. He asserted that the British Constitution was "grounded on the eternal and immutable laws of nature." It was a constitution "whose foundation and centre is liberty which sends liberty to every subject" within "its ample circumference."[22] Lord Camden took this kindly view of the Constitution as it stood, but others, radical reformers, like John Cartwright, recognized Parliament's absolutism and demanded reform. He held that the Constitution ought not to be easily changed from day to day, but "should be written and taught to children with the Lord's Prayer and the ten commandments."[23] In that way the limits of Parliament's power

over the individual would be known and every man could stoutly assert his own rights.

Men who thought with Lord Camden and John Cartwright were in the minority in England, while those who agreed with Adams and Otis were in the majority in America. Such a state of affairs menaced the unity of the empire. Though America and England had political principles and traditions springing from a common source, though they were wonderfully alike in their ideals of political liberty, and though they used common measures of social justice, yet historical chance and varied environment created differences in methods of attaining and enjoying political liberty which proved fatal to union. The contrast cannot be too strongly insisted upon. Samuel Adams and many of his fellow countrymen, on the one hand, believed that the British Constitution was fixed by "the law of God and nature," and founded in the principles of law and reason so that Parliament could not alter it,[24] but Lord Mansfield and his followers, on the other hand, asserted rightly that "the constitution of this country has been always in a moving state, either gaining or losing something," and "there are things even in Magna Charta which are not constitutional now" and others which an act of Parliament might change.[25] Between two such conceptions of the powers of government compromise was difficult to attain. It was best, doubtless, for the highest good of free institutions in the world that each idea should freely work out its logical destiny. Both had splendid possibilities in their ultimate forms. In these two concepts one detects the main difference between English governmental

21 Like Martin Howard, of Rhode Island, in "A Letter from a Gentleman at Halifax" (1765), who held that a colonist might question the justice of a measure of Parliament, but not its jurisdiction.

22 Hansard, *Parliamentary History*, XVI, 178.

23 Kent, *The English Radicals*, 70.

24 Wells, *Samuel Adams*, I, 75–97.

25 Hansard, *Parliamentary Debates*, XVI, 197.

ideas and those underlying principles which furnish the basis of the Constitution of the United States. In England all political power is in the hands of government, though the ministry which wields that power is easily overthrown by a dissatisfied people. In America, with its written constitutions and judicial review, all government is of limited authority, though its agents are not so quickly or easily displaced when not obedient to the will of the people. Each system has its merits, each its disadvantages. These were the ultimate ends to which differing ideals were carrying two great peoples, but the immediate result of these diverging opinions was alienation and war. These fundamental differences in political thinking made the colonists and the rulers of the mother country impatient and suspicious of each other when they began to dispute over questions like the Navigation Acts and the Stamp Act. Men who believed that Parliament had succeeded to the King's "divine right" could see only hysterical nonsense in the Massachusetts confession of faith of 1767. "The natural rights of the colonists," it ran, "we humbly conceive to be the same with those of all other British subjects and indeed of all mankind. The principal of these rights is to be 'free from any superior power on earth and not to be under the will or legislative authority of man, but to have only the law of nature for his rule.' In general, freedom of men under government is to have standing fundamental rules to live by, common to every one of that society and made by the legislative power erected in it, a liberty to follow my own will in all things where that rule prescribes not, and not to be subject to the inconstant, uncertain, unknown, arbitrary will of another man." Such talk was a mere flight of fancy the

legal advisers of the Crown would say, alarming even in a speculative book, but full of menace if indulged in by men who were responsible for the government of British subjects in an American province. And what did Christopher Gadsden mean by allusion to those "latent though inherent rights of society, which no climate, no time, no constitution, no contract can ever destroy or diminish"? To a mind that venerated the Constitution such ideas were poisonous, and pointed plainly to anarchy. Colony and mother country had drifted far apart when representative men from Massachusetts and South Carolina could give serious expression to ideas so shocking to typical members of Parliament. Such differences in ideals were as important causes of a breaking-up of the empire as more concrete matters like oppressive taxation. Daniel Webster only exaggerated the truth when he declared that the American colonists took arms against a preamble and fought eight years against a declaration. There was no ruinous material damage to America in the attempted taxation, but as John Dickinson said, "A free people can never be too quick in observing nor too firm in opposing the beginnings of alteration either in form or reality, respecting institutions formed for their security. The first kind of alteration leads to the last."[26] The Americans did not regard liberty as a mere comparative release from tyranny; but possessed, as Burke said, "a fierce spirit of liberty" stronger than in any other people of the earth, and yet it was a spirit that accorded with English principles and English ideas. On that very subject of taxes — in England too — the greatest spirits, Burke reminded Parlia-

[26] Lord Acton, *Essays on the French Revolution,* 25.

ment, had acted and suffered,[27] and yet the people of England had but gained the right to be taxed only by Parliament, while James Otis implied something more when he cried — "By the laws of God and nature, government must not raise taxes on the property of the people without the consent of the people or their deputies. There can be no prescription old enough to supersede the law of Nature and the grant of God Almighty, who has given all

men a right to be free."[28] It was because the British statesmen could not grasp the true meaning of such words, that their colonists in America, who at one time, in Franklin's words, "had been led by a thread, governed at the expense of only a little pen, ink and paper," were before long to be "kept in subjection only by forts, citadels, garrisons and armies."

[27] Burke, *Works*, II, 120.

[28] Lord Acton, *Essays on the French Revolution*, 24.

Lawrence Henry Gipson:

THE AMERICAN REVOLUTION AS AN AFTERMATH OF THE GREAT WAR FOR THE EMPIRE, 1754-1763

GREAT wars in modern times have too frequently been the breeders of revolution. The exhausting armed struggles in which France became engaged in the latter half of the eighteenth century led as directly to the French Revolution as did the First World War to the Russian Revolution; it may be said as truly that the American Revolution was an aftermath of the Anglo-French conflict in the New World carried on between 1754 and 1763. This is by no means to deny that other factors were involved in the launching of these revolutionary movements. Before proceeding with an analysis of the theme of this paper, however, it would

be well to consider the wording of the title given to it.*

Words may be used either to disguise or to distort facts as well as to clarify them, but the chief task of the historian is to illuminate the past. He is faced, therefore, with the responsibility of using only such words as will achieve this broad objective of his calling and to reject those that obscure or defeat it. For this reason "the French and Indian War," as a term descriptive of the conflict to which we

* This paper was read before the colonial history section of the American Historical Association in December 1948 at the Annual Meeting held in Washington.

Reprinted by permission from *Political Science Quarterly*, LXV, No. 1 (March, 1950).

have just referred, has been avoided in this essay as well as in the writer's series on the *British Empire before the American Revolution*. This has been done in spite of the fact that it has been employed by most Americans ever since the early days of our Republic and therefore has the sanction of long usage as well as the sanction of American national tradition assigning, as does the latter, to the Revolutionary War a position of such commanding importance as to make all other events in American history, preceding as well as following it, quite subordinate to it. In contrast to this traditional interpretation of our history one may affirm that the Anglo-French conflict settled nothing less than the incomparably vital question as to what civilization — what complex cultural patterns, what political institutions — would arise in the great Mississippi basin and the valleys of the rivers draining it, a civilization, whatever it might be, surely destined to expand to the Pacific seaboard and finally to dominate the North American continent. The determination of this crucial issue is perhaps the most momentous event in the life of the English-speaking people in the New World and quite overshadows in importance both the Revolutionary War and the later Civil War, events which, it is quite clear, were each contingent upon the outcome of the earlier crisis.

A struggle of such proportions, involving tremendous stakes, deserves a name accurately descriptive of its place in the history of the English-speaking people, and the title "the French and Indian War," as suggested, in no way fulfills this need. For the war was not, as the name would seem to imply, a conflict largely between English and French New World colonials and their Indian allies, nor was it localized in North America to the extent that the name would appear to indicate.

In contrast, it was waged both before and after an open declaration of war by the British and French nations with all their resources for nine years on three oceans, and much of the land washed by the waters of them, and it ultimately brought in both Spain, allied to France, and Portugal, allied to Great Britain. While it involved, it is true, as the name would connote, wilderness fighting, yet of equal, if not of greater, importance in assessing its final outcome was the pouring forth of Britain's financial resources in a vast program of shipbuilding, in the equipment and support of the British and colonial armies and the royal navy, and in the subsidization both of allies on the European continent and of the colonies in America. If it also involved the reduction of the fortress of Louisbourg, Fort Niagara, Fort Duquesne, Quebec and Montreal in North America, each in turn to fall to British regulars aided by American provincial troops, these successes, of great significance, were, in fact, really contingent upon the resounding British naval victories in the Mediterranean, off the Strait of Gibraltar, in the Bay of Biscay, and elsewhere, that brought about the virtual extinction of the French navy and merchant marine and thereby presented to France — seeking to supply her forces in Canada and elsewhere with adequate reinforcements and matériel — a logistical problem so insoluble as to spell the doom of her North American empire and of her possessions in India and elsewhere.

If the term "the French and Indian War" meets none of the requirements of accurate historical nomenclature, neither does the term "the Seven Years' War" — a name appropriately enough employed by historians to designate the mighty conflict that raged for seven years in Germany before its conclusion in the Treaty of Hubertusburg in 1763. The principals in this war were Prussia, allied with Great Britain, Hanover, Brunswick and Hesse, facing Austria, most of the Holy Roman Empire, Russia and Sweden, all allied with France and receiving subsidies from her. Although George II, as King of Great Britain and Elector of Hanover, in the treaty of 1758 with Frederick of Prussia, promised not to conclude peace without mutual agreement with the latter, and although large subsidies were annually paid to Prussia as well as to the other continental allies out of the British treasury and troops were also sent to Germany, it must be emphasized that these aids were designed primarily for the protection of the King's German Electorate. In other words, the British alliance in no way supported the objectives of the Prussian King, when he suddenly began the German war in 1756 by invading Saxony — two years after the beginning of the Anglo-French war. In this connection it should be borne in mind that throughout the Seven Years' War in Germany Great Britain remained at peace with both Russia and Sweden and refused therefore to send a fleet into the Baltic in spite of the demands of Frederick that this be done; nor were British land troops permitted to assist him against Austria, but only to help form a protective shield for Hanover against the thrusts of the French armies. For the latter were determined not only to overrun the Electorate — something that they succeeded in doing — but to hold it as a bargaining point to be used at the conclusion of hostilities with Great Britain, a feat, however, beyond their power of accomplishment. Closely related and intertwined as were the two wars, they were, nevertheless, distinct in their beginning and distinct in their termination.

Indeed, while British historians at length were led to adopt the nomenclature applied by German and other continental historians to all hostilities that took place between 1754 and 1763 in both the Old and New Worlds, American historians, by and large in the past, have rejected, and rightly so, it seems, the name "the Seven Years' War" to designate specifically the struggle during these years in North America with the fate of that continent at stake; so likewise many of them have rejected, as equally inadmissible, the name "the French and Indian War." Instead, the late Professor Osgood employed the title "the Fourth Intercolonial War," surely not a good one; George Bancroft called the war "the American Revolution: First Phase," still more inaccurate in some respects than the names he sought to avoid; Francis Parkman, with the flare of a romanticist, was at first inclined to call it "the Old French War" but finally, under the influence of the great-man-in-history thesis, gave to his two remarkable volumes concerned with it the totally misleading name, *Montcalm and Wolfe;* finally, John Fiske, the philosopher-historian, as luminous in his views as he was apt to be careless in the details of historical scholarship, happily fastened upon the name "the Great War." In the series on the *British Empire before the American Revolution* the writer has built upon Fiske's title and has called it "the Great War for the Empire" in order to emphasize not only the fact that the war was a very great conflict both in its scope and in its lasting effects, as Fiske saw it with clearness, but also, as a war entered into specifically for the defense of the British Empire, that it was by far the most important ever waged by Great Britain to this end.

It may be pointed out that later charges, especially by American writers, that the war was begun by Great Britain with less worthy motives in mind, are not supported by the great mass of state papers and the private correspondence of British statesmen responsible for making the weighty decisions at the time — materials now available to the student which the writer has attempted to analyze in detail in the two volumes of his series that appeared under the title of *Zones of International Friction, 1748–1754.* In other words, the idea that the war was started as the result of European balance-of-power politics or by British mercantilists for the purpose of destroying a commercial rival and for conquering Canada and the French West Indies, and for expelling the French from India, rather than for the much more limited and legitimate objective of affording the colonies and particularly the new province of Nova Scotia and the Old Dominion of Virginia protection against the aggressive aims of France, must be dismissed by students brought face to face with impressive evidence to the contrary.

The development of the war into one for the military mastery of the North American continent came with the growing conviction on the part of the British ministers that nothing short of this drastic step would realize the primary aims of the government in arriving at the determination, as the result of appeals from the colonies for assistance, to challenge the right of French troops to be planted well within the borders of the Nova Scotia peninsula and at the forks of the Ohio. One may go as far as to state that the acquisition of Canada — as an objective sought by mercantilists to contribute to the wealth of Great Britain — would have seemed fantastic to any contemporary who had the slightest knowledge of the tremendous financial drain that that great possession had been on the treasury of the French King for over a century before 1754.

Moreover, the motives that ultimately led, after much searching of heart, to its retention after its conquest by Great Britain were not commercial but strategic and had primarily in view the security and welfare generally of the older American colonies.

In view of these facts, not to be confused with surmises, the name "the Great War for the Empire" seems to the writer not only not inappropriate but among all the names heretofore applied to the war in question by far the most suitable that can be used by one concerned with the history of the old British Empire, who seeks earnestly to maintain that standard of exactness in terminology, as well as in other respects, which the public has a right to demand of him.

The description just given of the motives that led to the Great War for the Empire, nevertheless, runs counter, as suggested, to American national tradition and most history that has been written by American historians in harmony with it. This tradition had a curious beginning. It arose partly out of Pitt's zealous efforts to energize the colonies to prosecute the war most actively; but there also was another potent factor involved in its creation. Before the conclusion of hostilities in 1763 certain powerful commercial interests — centered particularly at Newport, Rhode Island, Boston, New York City, and to a less extent in Philadelphia — in a desire to continue an enormously lucrative trade with the French West Indies, and therefore with the enemy, all in the face of Pitt's determination to keep supplies from the French armed forces operating in the New World, began to express themselves in terms that implied that the war was peculiarly Great Britain's war and only incidentally one that concerned her colonies and that the French, really friendly to the aspirations of British colonials, were opposed only to the mercantilistic ambitions of the mother country. By 1766 — just twelve years after the beginning of the war and three years after its termination — this extraordinary tradition had become so well established that Benjamin Franklin, astonishingly enough, could actually assert in his examination before a committee of the House of Commons:

I know the last war is commonly spoke of here as entered into for the defence, or for the sake of the people of America; I think it is quite misunderstood. It began about the limits between Canada and Nova Scotia, about territories to which the crown indeed laid claim, but were not claimed by any British colony. . . . We had therefore no particular concern or interest in that dispute. As to the Ohio, the contest there began about your right of trading in the Indian country, a right you had by the Treaty of Utrecht, which the French infringed . . . they took a fort which a company of your merchants, and their factors and correspondents, had erected there to secure that trade. Braddock was sent with an army to retake that fort . . . and to protect your trade. It was not until after his defeat that the colonies were attacked. They were before in perfect peace with both French and Indians. . . .

By the beginning of 1768 the tradition had been so extended that John Dickinson — voicing the popular American view in his highly important *Letters from a Farmer in Pennsylvania,* No. VIII — felt that he not only could affirm, as did Franklin, that the war was strictly Britain's war and fought for selfish purposes, but could even insist that the acquisition of territory in North America as the result of it "is greatly injurious to these colonies" and that they therefore were not under the slightest obligation to the mother country.

But to return to the last phases of the Great War for the Empire. The British customs officials — spurred into unusual activity in the face of Pitt's demand for the strict enforcement of the Trade and Navigation Acts in order to break up the pernicious practice of bringing aid and comfort to the enemy — were led to employ writs of assistance for the purpose of laying their hands upon goods landed in American ports and secured in exchange for American provisions sent for the most part either directly or indirectly to the French West Indies. Although in the midst of hostilities, most of the merchants in Boston showed bitter opposition to the writs and equally ardent support of James Otis' declaration made in open court in 1761 that Parliament, acting within the limits of the constitution, was powerless to extend the use of these writs to America, whatever its authority might be in Great Britain. The importance of this declaration lies not so much in its immediate effect but rather in the fact that it was indicative of the line of attack that not only Otis would subsequently follow but also the Adamses, Hawley, Hancock, and other popular leaders in the Bay colony during the developing crisis, in the laying down of constitutional restrictions upon the power of Parliament to legislate for America. Further, it is clear that, even before the Great War for the Empire had been terminated, there were those in the province who had begun to view Great Britain as the real enemy rather than France.

Just as definitely as was the issue over writs of assistance related to the war under consideration was that growing out of the twopenny acts of the Virginia Assembly. In search of funds for maintaining the frontier defensive forces under the command of Colonel George Washington, the Assembly was led to pass in 1755 and 1758 those highly questionable laws as favorable to the tobacco planters as they were indefensibly unjust to the clergy. Even assuming the fact that these laws were war measures, and therefore in a sense emergency measures, it was inconceivable that the Privy Council would permit so palpable a violation of contractual relations as they involved. The royal disallowance of the laws in question opened the way for Patrick Henry, the year that hostilities were terminated by the Peace of Paris, not only to challenge in the Louisa County courthouse the right of the King in Council to refuse to approve any law that a colony might pass that in its judgment was a good law, but to affirm that such refusal was nothing less than an act of tyranny on the part of the King. It was thus resentment at the overturning of Virginia war legislation that led to this attack upon the judicial authority of review by the Crown — an authority exercised previously without serious protest for over a century. It should also be noted that the Henry thesis helped to lay the foundation for the theory of the equality of colonial laws with those passed by Parliament, a theory of the constitution of the empire that most American leaders in 1774 had come to accept in arguing that if the King could no longer exercise a veto over the acts of the legislature of Great Britain, it was unjust that he should do so over those of the colonial assemblies.

But the most fateful aftermath of the Great War for the Empire, with respect to the maintenance of the historic connection between the mother country and the colonies, grew out of the problem of the control and support not only of the vast trans-Appalachian interior, the right to which was now confirmed by treaty to Great Britain, but of the new acquisitions in North America secured from France and Spain. Under the terms of the royal Proclamation of 1763, French Canada to the east of the Great Lakes was organized as the Province of Quebec; most of old Spanish Florida became the Province of East Florida; and those areas, previously held by Spain as well as by France to the west of the Apalachicola and to the east of New Orleans and its immediate environs, became the Province of West Florida. The Proclamation indicated that proper inducements would be offered British and other Protestants to establish themselves in these new provinces. With respect to the trans-Appalachian region, however, it created there a temporary but vast Indian reserve by laying down as a barrier the crest of the mountains beyond which there should be no white settlement except by specific permission of the Crown.

The Proclamation has been represented not only as a blunder, the result largely of carelessness and ignorance on the part of those responsible for it, but also as a cynical attempt by the British ministry to embody mercantilistic principles in an American land policy that in itself ran counter to the charter limits of many of the colonies and the interests in general of the colonials. Nevertheless, this view of the Proclamation fails to take into account the fact that it was the offspring of the war and that the trans-Appalachian aspects of it were an almost inevitable result of promises made during the progress of hostilities. For both in the Treaty of Easton in 1758 with the Ohio Valley Indians, a treaty ratified by the Crown, and in the asseverations of such military leaders as Colonel Bouquet, these Indians were assured that they would be secure in their trans-Appalachian lands as a reward for deserting their allies, the French. As a sign of good faith, the lands lying within the bounds of Pennsylvania to the west of the mountains, purchased by the Proprietors from the Six Nations in 1754, were solemnly released. Thus committed in honor in the course of the war, what could the Cabinet Council at its termination do other than it finally did in the Proclamation of 1763? But this step not only was in opposition to the interests of such groups of land speculators as, for example, the Patrick Henry group in Virginia and the Richard Henderson group in North Carolina, both of whom boldly ignored the Proclamation in negotiating with the Cherokee Indians for land grants, but also led to open defiance of this imperial regulation by frontiersmen who, moving beyond the mountains by the thousands, proceeded to settle within the Indian reserve — some on lands previously occupied before the beginning of the late war or before the great Indian revolt in 1763, and others on new lands.

The Proclamation line of 1763 might have become an issue, indeed a most formidable one, between the government of Great Britain and the colonials, had not the former acquiesced in the inevitable and confirmed certain Indian treaties that provided for the transfer of much of the land which had been the particular object of quest on the part of speculators and of those moving westward from the settled areas to establish new homes. Such were the treaties of Hard Labor, Fort Stanwix, Lochaber, and the modification of the last-named by the Donelson agreement with the Cherokees in 1771. Nor did the regulation of the trans-Appalachian Indian trade create serious colonial irritation, especially in view of the failure of the government to implement the elaborate Board of Trade plan drawn up in 1764. The same, however, cannot be said of the program put forward by the ministry and accepted by Parliament for securing the means to maintain order and provide protection for this vast area and the new acquisitions to the north and south of it.

Theoretically, it would have been possible for the government of Great Britain to have dropped onto the lap of the old continental colonies the entire responsibility for maintaining garrisons at various strategic points in North America — in Canada, about the Great Lakes, in the Ohio and Mississippi valleys, and in East and West Florida. In spite, however, of assertions made by some prominent colonials, such as Franklin, in 1765 and 1766, that the colonies would be able and were willing to take up the burden of providing for the defense of America, this, under the circumstances, was utterly chimerical, involving, as it would have, not only a vast expenditure of funds but highly complicated inter-colonial arrangements, even in the face of the most serious inter-colonial rivalry such as that between Pennsylvania and Virginia respecting the control of the upper Ohio Valley. The very proportions of the task were an insuperable obstacle to leaving it to the colonies; and the colonies, moreover, would have been faced by another impediment almost as difficult to surmount — the utter aversion of Americans of the eighteenth century, by and large, to the dull routine of garrison duty. This was emphasized by the Massachusetts Bay Assembly in 1755 in its appeal to the government of Great Britain after Braddock's defeat to send regulars to man the frontier forts of that province; the dispatches of Colonel George Washington in 1756 and in 1757 respecting the shameful desertion of militiamen, ordered to hold the chain of posts on the western frontier of Virginia in order to check the frightful French and Indian raids, support this position, as does the testimony in 1757 of Governor Lyttelton of South Carolina, who made clear that the inhabitants of that colony were not at all adapted to this type of work. The postwar task of garrison duty was clearly one to be assumed by regulars held to their duty under firm discipline and capable of being shifted from one strategic point to another as circumstances might require. Further, to be effective, any plan for the defense of the new possessions and the trans-Appalachian region demanded unity of command, something the colonies could not provide. Manifestly this could be done only through the instrumentalities of the mother country.

The British ministry, thus confronted with the problem of guaranteeing the necessary security for the extended empire in North America, which it was estimated would involve the annual expenditure of from three to four hundred thousand pounds for the maintenance of ten thousand troops — according to various estimates made by General Amherst and others in 1764 and to be found among the Shelburne Papers — was impelled to raise the question: Should not the colonials be expected to assume some definite part of the cost of this? In view of the fact that it was felt not only that they were in a position to do so but that the stability of these outlying possessions was a matter of greater concern and importance generally to them, by reason of their proximity, than to the people of the mother country three thousand miles away, the answer was in the affirmative. The reason for this is not hard to fathom. The nine years of war had involved Britons in tremendous expenditures. In spite of very heavy taxation during these years, the people were left saddled at the termination of hostilities with a national debt of unprecedented proportions for that day and age of over one hundred and forty million pounds. It was necessary not only to service and to retire this debt, in so far as was possible, but also to meet the ordinary demands of the civil government and to maintain the navy at a point of strength that would offer some assurance that France and Spain would have no desire in the future to plan a war to recover their territorial losses. In addition to all this, there was now the problem of meeting the charges necessary for keeping the new possessions in North America under firm military control for their internal good order and for protection from outside interference.

It may be noted that before the war the British budget had called for average annual expenditures of six and a half million pounds; between the years 1756 and 1766 these expenditures mounted to fourteen and a half million pounds a year on the average and from the latter date to 1775 ranged close to ten million pounds. As a result, the annual per capita tax in Great Britain, from 1763 to 1775, without considering local rates, was many times the average annual per capita tax in even those American colonies that made the greatest contribution to the Great War for the Empire, such as Massachusetts Bay and Connecticut — without reference to those colonies that had done little or nothing in this conflict, and therefore had accumulated little in the way of a war debt, such as Maryland and Georgia. The student of the history of the old British Empire, in fact, should accept with great reserve statements to the contrary — some of them quite irresponsible in nature — made by Americans during the heat of the controversy, with respect to the nature of the public burdens they were obliged to carry in the years preceding the outbreak of the

Revolutionary War. In this connection a study of parliamentary reimbursement of colonial war expenses from 1756 to 1763 in its relation to public debts in America between the years 1763 and 1775 is most revealing. As to American public finance, all that space will here permit is to state that there is abundant evidence to indicate that, during the five-year period preceding the outbreak of the Revolutionary War, had the inhabitants of any of the thirteen colonies, which therefore included those of Massachusetts Bay and Virginia, been taxed in one of these years at the average high per capita rate that the British people were taxed from 1760 to 1775, the proceeds of that one year's tax not only would have taken care of the ordinary expenditures of the colony in question for that year but also would have quite liquidated its war debt, so little of which remained in any of the colonies by 1770. Well may John Adams have admitted in 1780 what was equally true in 1770: "America is not used to great taxes, and the people there are not yet disciplined to such enormous taxation as in England."

Assuming, as did the Grenville ministry in 1764, the justice of expecting the Americans to share in the cost of policing the new possessions in North America, the simplest and most obvious way, it might appear, to secure this contribution to a common end so important to both Americans and Britons was to request the colonial governments to make definite grants of funds. This was the requisition or quota system that had been employed in the course of the recent war. But the most obvious objections to it were voiced that same year by Benjamin Franklin, who, incidentally, was to reverse himself the following year in conferring with

Grenville as the Pennsylvania London agent. In expressing confidentially his personal, rather than any official, views to his friend Richard Jackson on June 25, 1764 he declared: "Quota's would be difficult to settle at first with Equality, and would, if they could be made equal at first, soon become unequal, and never would be satisfactory." Indeed, experience with this system in practice, as a settled method of guaranteeing even the minimum essential resources for the end in view, had shown its weakness and utter unfairness. If it could not work equitably even in war time, could it be expected to work in peace? It is, therefore, not surprising that this method of securing even a portion of the funds required for North American security should have been rejected in favor of some plan that presented better prospects of a definite American revenue.

The plan of last resort to the ministry was therefore to ask Parliament to act. That Grenville, however, was aware that serious objections might be raised against any direct taxation of the colonials by the government of Great Britain is indicated by the caution with which he approached the solution of the problem of securing from America about a third of the total cost of its defense. The so-called Sugar Act first of all was passed at his request. This provided for import duties on certain West Indian and other products. Colonial import duties imposed by Parliament, at least since 1733, were no innovation. But the anticipated yield of these duties fell far short of the desired one hundred thousand pounds. He therefore, in introducing the bill for the above Act, raised the question of a stamp duty but requested postponement of parliamentary action until the colonial governments had been consulted. The latter were thereupon requested to make any suggestions for ways of raising an American fund that might seem more proper to the people than such a tax. Further, it would appear — at least, according to various London advices published in Franklin and Hall's *Pennsylvania Gazette* — that proposals were seriously considered by the Cabinet Council during the fall of 1764 for extending to the colonies representation in Parliament through the election of members to the House of Commons by various colonial assemblies. However, it is quite clear that by the beginning of 1765 any such proposals, as seem to have been under deliberation by the ministry, had been put aside when Grenville at length had become convinced that representation in Parliament was neither actively sought nor even desired by Americans. For the South Carolina Commons House of Assembly went strongly on record against this idea in September 1764 and was followed by the Virginia House of Burgesses in December. In fact, when in the presence of the London colonial agents the minister had outlined the objections raised by Americans to the idea of such representation, no one of them, including Franklin, was prepared to deny the validity of these objections. That he was not mistaken in the opposition of Americans at large to sending members to Parliament, in spite of the advocacy of this by James Otis, is clear in the resolutions passed both by other colonial assemblies than the ones to which reference has been made and by the Stamp Act Congress in 1765. Indeed, in 1768 the House of Representatives of Massachusetts Bay went so far in its famous Circular Letter framed in opposition to the Townshend duties as to make clear that the people of that colony actually preferred taxation by Parliament

without representation to such taxation with representation.

When — in view of the failure of the colonial governments to suggest any practicable, alternate plan for making some contribution to the post-war defensive program in North America — Grenville finally urged in Parliament the passage of an American stamp bill, he acted on an unwarranted assumption. This assumption was — in paraphrasing the minister's remarks to the colonial agents in 1765 — that opposition to stamp taxes, for the specific purpose in mind, would disappear in America both in light of the benefits such provision would bring to colonials in general and by reason of the plain justice of the measure itself; and that, in place of opposition, an atmosphere of mutual goodwill would be generated by a growing recognition on the part of Americans that they could trust the benevolence of the mother country to act with fairness to all within the empire. Instead, with the news of the passage of the act, cries of British tyranny and impending slavery soon resounded throughout the entire eastern Atlantic American seaboard. What would have been the fate of the empire had Grenville remained in office to attempt to enforce the act, no one can say. But as members of the opposition to the Rockingham ministry, he and his brother, Earl Temple, raised their voices — one as a commoner, the other as a peer — in warning that the American colonies would inevitably be lost to the empire should Parliament be led to repeal the act in the face of colonial resistance and the pressure of British merchants. Had Parliament determined, in spite of violence and threats of violence, to enforce the act, it might have meant open rebellion and civil war, ten years before it actually occurred. Instead, this body decided to yield and, in spite of the passing of the so-called Declaratory Act setting forth its fundamental powers to legislate on all matters relating to the empire, suffered a loss of prestige in the New World that was never to be regained.

But the Stamp Act was not the sole object of attack by colonials. To many of them not only the Sugar Act of 1764 but the whole English pre-war trade and navigation system was equally, if not actually more, obnoxious. Indeed, the unusual energy displayed by the navy and the customs officials, spurred into action by Pitt during the latter years of the war — bringing with it the condemnation in courts of vice-admiralty of many American vessels whose owners were guilty of serious trade violations, if not greater crimes — generated a degree of antagonism against the whole body of late seventeenth- and early eighteenth-century restrictions on commercial intercourse such as never had previously existed. It is not without significance that the greatest acts of terrorism and destruction during the great riot of August 1765 in Boston were directed not against the Massachusetts Bay stamp distributor but against those officials responsible for encouraging and supporting the enforcement, during the late war, of the various trade acts passed long before its beginning in 1754. The hatred also of the Rhode Island merchants, as a group, against the restrictions of the navigation system as well as against the Sugar Act of 1764, remained constant. Moreover, in December 1766 most of the New York merchants, over two hundred in number, showed their repugnance to the way that this system was functioning by a strongly worded petition to the House of Commons in which they enumerated an impressive list of grievances that they asked

to be redressed. Even Chatham, the great friend of America, regarded their petition "highly improper: in point of time most absurd, in the extent of their pretensions, most excessive; and in the reasoning, most grossly fallacious and offensive." In fact, all the leading men in Great Britain supported the system of trade restrictions.

Nevertheless, the determination of the government — in view especially of the great financial burdens that the late war had placed upon the mother country — to enforce it now much more effectively than had been done before 1754, and to that end in 1767 to pass appropriate legislation in order to secure funds from the colonies by way of import duties so that public officials in America might be held to greater accountability when paid their salaries by the Crown, could have only one result: the combined resistance of those, on the one hand, opposed to any type of taxation that Parliament might apply to America and of those, on the other, desiring to free the colonies of hampering trade restrictions.

The suggestion on the part of the Continental Congress in 1774 that Americans would uphold the British navigation system, if exempted from parliamentary taxation, while a shrewd gesture to win support in England, had really, it would seem, no other significance. For it is utterly inconceivable that the Congress itself, or the individual colonial governments, could have set up machinery capable of preventing violations of the system at will on the part of those whose financial interests were adversely affected by its operation. Moreover, it is obvious that, by the time the news had reached America that Lord North's ministry had secured the passage of the coercive acts — for the most part directed against Massachusetts Bay for the defiant destruction of the East India Company's tea — leading colonials, among them Franklin, had arrived at the conclusion that Parliament possessed powers so very limited with respect to the empire that without the consent of the local assemblies it could pass neither constitutional nor fiscal legislation that affected Americans and the framework of their governments. It is equally obvious that this represented a most revolutionary position when contrasted with that held by Franklin and the other delegates to the Albany Congress twenty years earlier. For it was in 1754 that the famous Plan of Union was drawn up there and approved by the Congress — a plan based upon the view that Parliament, and not the Crown, had supreme authority within the empire, an authority that alone was adequate in view of framers of the Plan to bring about fundamental changes in the constitutions of the colonies in order legally to clothe the proposed union government with adequate fiscal as well as other powers.

In accounting for the radical change in attitude of many leading colonials between the years 1754 and 1774 respecting the nature of the constitution of the empire, surely among the factors that must be weighed was the truly overwhelming victory achieved in the Great War for the Empire. This victory not only freed colonials for the first time in the history of the English-speaking people in the New World from dread of the French, their Indian allies, and the Spaniards, but, what is of equal significance, opened up to them the prospect, if given freedom of action, of a vast growth of power and wealth with an amazing westward expansion. Indeed, it is abundantly clear that a continued subordination of the colonies to the government of Great Britain was no longer considered an asset in

the eyes of many Americans by 1774, as it had been so judged by them to be in 1754, but rather an onerous liability. What, pray tell, had the debt-ridden mother country to offer in 1774 to the now geographically secure, politically mature, prosperous, dynamic, and self-reliant offspring along the Atlantic seaboard, except the dubious opportunity of accepting new, as well as retaining old, burdens? And these burdens would have to be borne in order to lighten somewhat the great financial load that the taxpayers of Great Britain were forced to carry by reason of obligations the nation had assumed both in the course of the late war and at its termination. If many Americans thought they had a perfect right to profit personally by trading with the enemy in time of war, how much more deeply must they have resented in time of peace the serious efforts made by the home government to enforce the elaborate restrictions on commercial intercourse? Again, if, even after the defeat of Colonel Washington at Great Meadows in 1754, colonials such as Franklin were opposed to paying any tax levied by Parliament for establishing a fund for the defense of North America, how much more must they have been inclined to oppose such taxation to that end with the passing in 1763 of the great international crisis?

At this point the question must be frankly faced: If France had won the war decisively and thereby consolidated her position and perfected her claims in Nova Scotia, as well as to the southward of the St. Lawrence, in the Great Lakes region, and in the Ohio and Mississippi valleys, is it at all likely that colonials would have made so fundamental a constitutional issue of the extension to them of the principle of the British stamp tax? Would they have resisted such a tax had

Parliament imposed it in order to provide on an equitable basis the maximum resources for guaranteeing their safety, at a time when they were faced on their highly restricted borders by a militant, victorious enemy having at its command thousands of ferocious redskins? Again, accepting the fact of Britain's victory, is it not reasonable to believe that, had Great Britain at the close of the triumphant war left Canada to France and carefully limited her territorial demands in North America to those comparatively modest objectives that she had in mind at its beginning, there would have been no very powerful movement within the foreseeable future toward complete colonial autonomy — not to mention American independence? Would not Americans have continued to feel the need as in the past to rely for their safety and welfare upon British sea power and British land power, as well as upon British resources generally? In other words, was Governor Thomas Hutchinson of Massachusetts Bay far mistaken when, in analyzing the American situation late in 1773, he affirmed in writing to the Earl of Dartmouth:

Before the peace [of 1763] I thought nothing so much to be desired as the cession of Canada. I am now convinced that if it had remained to the French none of the spirit of opposition to the Mother Country would have yet appeared & I think the effects of it [that is, the cession of Canada] worse than all we had to fear from the French or Indians.

In conclusion, it may be said that it would be idle to deny that most colonials in the eighteenth century at one time or another felt strongly the desire for freedom of action in a wider variety of ways than was legally permitted before 1754. Indeed, one can readily uncover these strong impulses even in the early part of the seventeenth century. Yet Americans were, by and large, realists, as were the British, and under the functioning of the imperial system from, let us say, 1650 to 1750 great mutual advantages were enjoyed, with a fair division, taking everything into consideration, of the financial burdens necessary to support the system. However, the mounting Anglo-French rivalry in North America from 1750 onward, the outbreak of hostilities in 1754, and the subsequent nine years of fighting destroyed the old equilibrium, leaving the colonials after 1760 in a highly favored position in comparison with the taxpayers of Great Britain. Attempts on the part of the Crown and Parliament to restore by statute the old balance led directly to the American constitutional crisis, out of which came the Revolutionary War and the establishment of American independence. Such, ironically, was the aftermath of the Great War for the Empire, a war that Britons believed, as the Earl of Shelburne affirmed in 1762 in Parliament, was begun for the "security of the British colonies in N. America. . . ."

James Truslow Adams:

THE ROLE OF MERCHANTS AND RADICALS IN THE REVOLUTIONARY MOVEMENT

EXCEPT for sections on the frontier which suffered from Indian raids, the colonies had not been the seat of any of the military operations of the Seven Years' War, which ended, as far as America was concerned, in 1760. As always happens in a war, a good many new fortunes had been built up. Privateering frequently proved exceedingly profitable, and the great prizes brought in encouraged speculation. Army contracts — such, for example, as one for two million pounds of beef and two million pounds of bread, among other supplies — lined the pockets of the contractors, who always emerge rich from such troubled periods. Business of all sorts had come to be conducted on a much larger scale, and we can clearly trace the growing connection between business leaders and subservient or participating legislatures, even one so close to the people as that of Connecticut. Lawyers were rising into prominence as business affairs became larger and more complex, and they also began to appear in legislatures.

For a while the farming and laboring classes had shared in the war-time prosperity; the farmer had got war-time prices and the laborer's wages had risen rapidly as the scarcity of labor had increased and floods of paper money had worked their usual inflation. But when the bubble broke, all of these classes suffered severely. Taxes had risen rapidly with the debts contracted by the several colonies. The currency became heavily depreciated. General business fell off sharply. The price of farm produce crashed. Many of the laborers and farmers had to abandon their homes. There was a severe decline in the price of farm land in the older settlements, many foreclosures of mortgages, lawsuits for debts which wiped out all equities. Once more the frontier seemed to offer the only hope to many of the poor who could not weather the storm.

But in 1763 came a stunning blow. England by proclamation forbade any colonials to cross the watershed of the mountains to settle. This was the British government's solution of the Indian problem, one of the first which required to be settled with respect to the new Canadian and western territory. The Ministers feared — not without good cause, as Pontiac's conspiracy was to show — that, with the savages already hostile to the English régime and perhaps stirred up by the French, there would be constant trouble on the frontier if the settlers pressed into the Indian hunting grounds. The valuable fur trade had to be preserved, and England had no wish to garrison a frontier of perhaps twelve hundred miles. As a temporary expedient, the government lit upon the idea of holding back immigration to the western country, and, in order to keep the Indians quiet, to erect for the present a large Indian territory. Unfortunately, with the procrastination in government affairs characteristic of the times, what was intended to be only a temporary expedient was never seriously considered again. The Americans felt that they had given considerable help in conquering America from the French, and were furious at being told that they must not enter the promised land. The population was doubling every twenty to twenty-five years. The post-war suffering was keenly felt. Canute might as well have commanded the waves not to advance as for the British government to forbid the Americans, in their distress, to seek new fortune across the mountains — except that the waves would not have resented it, whereas the colonists did.

We have already seen that there was plenty of resentment on the frontier in any case — resentment against New England land speculators, against the all-engrossing land-grabbers in New York, against the new slavocracy in the South; resentment on the part of the new immigrants against those who had cheated and ill-used them; resentment against the landlords of England by the Scotch-Irish. Typical of the feeling of the latter was the inscription that was carved on the tombstone of one of them in the Shenandoah Valley. "Here lies," so it read, "the remains of John Lewis, who slew the Irish Lord, settled Augusta County, located the town of Staunton, and furnished five sons to fight the battles of the American Revolution." There is ample evidence that the frontier was full of combustible material — lawless, resentful, radical, and independent. Moreover, in the older settlements the poorer people were full of trouble and grievances at this time and quite ready to father them upon anyone. Even the

rich were beginning to feel hard times. If more grievances came, it would not be very difficult to stir sedition into a flame. There was a flare-up in 1761 when the Courts in Boston were asked by the revenue officers to issue new "writs of assistance," all the old ones having expired with the death of George II. These were of the nature of general search warrants, not naming the particular place to be searched or the object to be searched for, and had been used for some years, at the suggestion of Pitt, chiefly to try to prevent the illicit trade between Boston merchants and the French enemy, which had been prolonging the war. James Otis, who argued against them in a fiery speech, although he lost his case, took the proper ground that they were destructive of liberty, and John Adams once said that the American Revolution began then and there.

The first move made by the English government to reorganize the administration of the empire was along the lines of old legislation accepted by the colonists in principle though not complied with in practice. In 1764, in an effort to secure some customs revenue, which heretofore had sufficed only to pay a quarter of the cost of collection, the Sugar Act was passed by Parliament, followed by two others in the next two years.

These three Acts might have seriously demoralized commerce, but as their incidence happened to be almost wholly on the trade carried on by New England, the issue was not felt by all the colonies. The Stamp Act in 1765, however, as being internal taxation, affected every colony alike, though not to equal extent financially, as did also the Townshend Acts of 1767, which included duties on imports of manufactured articles from Great Britain. Moreover, both these last were especially designed to transfer a revenue from the colonies in sterling or bills of exchange, when it was difficult enough to find sufficient of either to make good the annual adverse balance of trade. They also marked a new sort of legislation, different from the mere trade regulation of old.

The excitement during these years was intense. The economic structure of the colonies, already seriously affected, was threatened with ruin. Business grew rapidly worse, and the passage of the Stamp Act had given a focus for every possible form of discontent. The reaction expressed in varying tones from Patrick Henry's well-known speech up to the dignified papers drawn up by representatives of the various colonies in the Stamp Act Congress, as well as the mobbing and burning of houses in various towns, made the British government realize it had gone too far as a matter of expediency. Both the Sugar Act and the Stamp Act were soon repealed, and in 1770, after a non-importation agreement, enforced in the colonies, had reduced imports from Great Britain by nearly half, the Townshend Acts also were largely modified, leaving only a trifling tax on tea as a symbol of the power of Parliament. The much disliked Act quartering British soldiers on the colonists where garrisons were maintained was also allowed to lapse without being reënacted. The British government pledged itself to attempt to raise no further revenue in America; the non-importation agreements were rescinded; and American imports from England rose from £1,634,000 in 1769 to £4,200,000 in 1771. Here and there in various colonies there were local grievances against England, but prosperity had returned to America, and the wealthy, as well as many of the classes dependent on them, were inclined to for-

get the quarrel with the mother country.

Meanwhile, however, much that was ominous for the future had happened. The merchant and other wealthy and conservative classes had been chiefly anxious to avoid trouble and merely to get the obnoxious acts rescinded. The English mind which America inherited has nearly always preferred adjustment and working compromises to declarations of abstract principles. The wealthy men had been willing to fight their cause on the grounds that the new laws were inexpedient and that they would damage the business interests of England as well as their own, a line of argument in which they received the cordial support of the mercantile interests in London who did business with them, and who agreed with their point of view. In fact, the repeal of the various acts was due more to the English mercantile influence brought to bear on Parliament than to either the mobbing or the constitutional arguments in America. What the English merchants and the richer men in the colonies wanted above all was good business and as little political friction as possible.

On the other hand, as we have seen, there was a vast mass of smouldering discontent among the poorer people everywhere in America. The line of economic class cleavage was beginning to be more clearly defined, and the lower in the scale were beginning to look to men from among their own ranks to lead them politically. When, for example, Patrick Henry tried to secure the passage of his Stamp Act resolutions in the Virginia House of Burgesses, he was unanimously backed by the poor electors, whereas he had to overcome the almost solid resistance of the rich. However, the greatest master in manipulating the masses whom America has ever seen, except possibly Bryan, arose in Boston.

Opinions will always differ regarding Samuel Adams, but there can be no difference of opinion as to his consummate ability as a plotter of revolution. In all else he was a failure throughout his life. Before the years in which his manipulation of the inflammable material among the public was to give him a lasting place in American history, he had failed in law and business and public office. In after years, when constructive work had to be done in Congress in constitution making or as governor of his new State, he played a wholly insignificant part. He could tear down, but not build up. He was a fanatic, as most men are who change history, and with a fanatical hatred of England he strove to break all ties with her. Had he lived a century earlier he would have been one of the stern Puritan leaders of the type of Endicott, unyielding, persecuting, convinced to the very marrow of his bones of the infallibility of his own beliefs. But although he was a Puritan of the Puritans, the times had changed. They had become political, and in Adams's mind England and her rule had become the principle of evil in the lives of the people of God, to be fought day and night and with every weapon in his arsenal. Even when others had no wish to secede from the empire, but merely to be left in peace or to have certain inimical laws repealed, Adams early conceived the belief that the one end to work for was immediate and complete independence.

As he surveyed the field of public opinion in which he would have to operate, he saw clearly the two classes of rich and poor and realized that their interests were different. The rich were conservative, the poor radical; the rich were desirous of as little change as possible, the poor clamored for any change that would better their condition; the rich would be influenced mainly by arguments of compromise and expediency, the poor by appeals to their rights for a greater share in the political and economic life of their communities. If these two classes could be brought to work together, public opinion would be a unit, but if they could not, then the greater reliance must be placed on the poorer classes, who constituted the overwhelming mass of the population and who could more readily be stirred to anger and radical action. From about 1761 until independence was declared by the colonies in 1776, Adams worked ceaselessly for the cause to which he had devoted his life, manipulating newspapers and town meetings, organizing committees for correspondence throughout the colonies, even bringing about happenings which would inflame public opinion. At one period it looked as though his efforts would be in vain, but in the end the stupidity of the British government won the day for him.

It is a great mistake to think of public opinion as united in the colonies and as gradually rising against British tyranny. Public opinion is never wholly united, and seldom rises to a pitch of passion without being influenced — in other words, without the use of propaganda. The Great War taught that to those who did not know it already.

The years preceding the final secession of the colonies may be divided into three periods. During the first, from the passage of the Sugar Act to the practical repeal of all obnoxious legislation in 1770, the different groups were by force of circumstances united in opposition to the policy of England. The merchants needed no propaganda to realize that their business was being seriously interfered with, though they cared little about the popular catchwords that were being used by the new leaders of the people to inflame them. The Stamp Act, however, with its threat of internal taxation, did, during its one brief year of life, bring the whole problem for a while from the realm of mere business to that of constitutional questioning. But by 1770 the merchants' grievances were settled, and from then until 1773 all desire for agitation and "rocking the boat" disappeared among the richer classes. Up to that point, the popular anger had served their own cause. For the next three years their cause was peace, and popular agitation and attacks on England became a menace and not a help to them.

From the first, Adams and those working with him had realized the necessity of democratic slogans in the creation of a state of mind. While the merchants were busy pointing out to their London correspondents that the new laws would hurt the business of all alike, Adams at once struck boldly out to inflame the passions of the crowd by threatening that it was to be reduced to the "miserable state of tributary slaves," contrasting its freedom and moral virtue with the tyranny and moral degradation of England. He proclaimed that the mother country was bent on bringing her colonies to a condition of "slavery, poverty and misery," and on causing their utter ruin, and dinned into the ears of the people the words "slavery and tyranny" until they assumed a reality from mere reiteration. His political philosophy was eagerly lapped up by a populace smarting under hard times and resentful of colonial even more than imperial conditions of the moment. The establishment of government by free consent of all had become imbedded in the mind of the average man, as an essential part of the American dream. Adams himself had seen the vision, but had glimpsed it with the narrowness and bitterness with which

the more bigoted Puritans had seen the vision of an unloving and revengeful Hebrew Jehovah. Like them he felt that he alone, and those who believed as he did, were in possession of the truth, and that those who differed from him were enemies of truth and God. Because, however, the American dream had so deeply affected the hopes and aspirations of the common men, the more radical among them, in town and on frontier, echoed with wild enthusiasm such pronouncements of Adams as that "the natural liberty of man is to be free from any superior power on earth, and not to be under the will or legislative authority of man, but only to have the law of nature for his rule."

Such talk as this could only make England fearful of how far the people might try to put such precepts into practice. The upper classes in the colonies also began to be uneasy. Up to 1770, when their own grievances were redressed, they might allow such ideas to be disseminated, considering themselves in control of the situation, but after that it became clear that they were losing control. Whereas such men as John Hancock and John Adams wanted quiet, and retired from public affairs to the management of their own, Sam Adams and the lesser radicals worked harder than ever to keep public opinion inflamed.

With the upper classes become lukewarm or hostile to his continued propaganda, with the obnoxious legislation repealed or modified, he had to trust to generalizations and emotional appeals. A good example of his use of the latter was the affair called the "Boston Massacre." As part of the general imperial policy following the war, the British government had stationed some regiments in Boston. They were under good officers and good discipline, and there was no more reason why they should have made trouble there than in any provincial garrison town of England. Adams, however, was continually stirring up the public mind against them; John Adams reported finding him one Sunday night "preparing for the next day's newspaper — a curious employment, cooking up paragraphs, articles, occurrences, etc., working the political engine." Finally, one March evening, as a result of more than usual provocation given by taunting boys to soldiers on duty, an unfortunate clash occurred. There was confusion, a rioter's shout to "fire" was mistaken for an officer's command, and several citizens were killed. The officer surrendered to the civil authorities, was tried, defended by John Adams and Josiah Quincy, Jr., and acquitted. But Samuel Adams at once saw the value of the incident. Every emotion of the mob was played upon. The affair was termed a "massacre," and in the annual speeches given for a number of years to commemorate its anniversary the boys and men who had taken part in the mobbing were described as martyrs to liberty and the soldiers as "bloody butchers." Although there is no recorded instance of a soldier having offered the slightest affront to any Boston girl, orators ranted about "our beauteous virgins exposed to all the insolence of unbridled passion — our virtuous wives, endeared to us by every tender tie, falling a sacrifice to worse than brutal violence, and perhaps, like the famed Lucretia, distracted with anguish and despair, ending their wretched lives by their own fair hands." At the request of the citizens the troops were removed from the city, but such talk, which served its intended purpose, was kept up for years after. The incident was unimportant in itself, and its chief interest is in how the radicals,

after having provoked it, made use of it.

America was, indeed, more or less in ferment, quite aside from the question of Anglo-American relations. Pennsylvania was almost on the verge of civil war, feeling having become extremely embittered between the older and newer sections of the colony. The rich seaboard counties had not only been unwilling to help protect the frontier in the late war, but were controlling all the political machinery for their own benefit, the sixteen thousand voters in the three eastern counties having twice as many members of the Assembly as the fifteen thousand in the five western counties. To some extent the mechanics in Philadelphia were making common cause with the frontiersmen against the moneyed class. In Virginia, there was similar feeling between classes and sections, the tidewater counties controlling the much more populous frontier ones. In North Carolina, civil war did actually break out after several years of agitation, and the frontiersmen set up their own organization of "Regulators" to prevent, among other things, the collection of taxes by the men of the eastern counties who controlled the legislature and graft of the colony, and who succeeded in putting down the insurrection only after three years' effort ending in a bloody campaign in 1772.

The Seven Years' War had left society disorganized and unstable. The rich, from 1764 to 1770, had their grievances against England, grievances that were real and deep, but they were also beginning to watch with alarm the rise of radical sentiment among their own people. Everywhere thoughtful, farseeing men were thinking — thinking of the constitutional relations with the mother country which had permitted so serious a crisis to arise as that from which they believed they had just happily emerged; thinking also of the problems of government in the colonies and of what might be in store for conservatism and wealth if the people, by continuing to press their demands for greater share in ruling themselves, should oust their old leaders who had been used to being in control. The more they pondered the Anglo-American constitutional relation, however, the more it became apparent that if the question should ever have to be forced to an issue, the only ground to take would be the broad one of the rights of man as man. Sam Adams was right in that. They had tried to argue from charter rights, and soon found that ground too narrow. Their rights as Englishmen afforded a wider scope, but argument thence tended toward a bog of legalistic confusion. If Parliament should try inimical legislation again, and if a situation should arise calling for a denial of its power to legislate, the broadest rights of man would be none too broad to provide standing room for argument. But this would play right into the hands of the discontented populace, who were already getting too obstreperous, demanding new rights, asking more representation, refusing to pay taxes, getting a bit too much into the habit of backing up their demands by mobbing, even plunging a colony like North Carolina into civil war. It was all bad for business, thought the rich, and holding back the development of the country. However, the quarrel with England was made up for the present. English merchants had seen the light. Perhaps, with better times in America, these agitations on the frontiers and by the lower classes in the big towns would die down, if only men like Sam Adams would know when to stop and would quit throwing oil on the flames. The rich determined to sit on the

lid, and carry out a policy of business and politics as usual. Sam Adams and his group also continued their agitation as usual.

For three years, from 1770, in spite of constant discussion in pamphlets and newspapers and declaimings by radicals, things seemed to be getting better. The frontiersmen and town radicals were doing a lot of talking, but getting nowhere. The Regulators' insurrection had been put down. Then suddenly the British government made a colossal blunder which could never be retrieved. Sam Adams saw to that.

The East India Company had accumulated a huge and partly unsalable store of tea, and was on the brink of bankruptcy. In order to prevent the catastrophe, which would have been a financial one of the first magnitude, the British government, with perfectly good intentions from an English point of view, but with an ignorance and a carelessness which are beyond condonation, gave the India Company what was practically a monopoly of selling tea in America. By the elimination of the American merchants as middlemen, the price of tea to the American consumer was expected to be cut in half; but considering the delicacy of Anglo-American relations, and the fact that the American merchant and business class was the chief reliance of England in America, to have struck a blow at it in favor of an English business concern revealed in a flash both the stupidity of the men in power with whom Americans had to deal and the unthinking selfishness of English policy with regard to the colonies. The fat was in the fire now with a vengeance. For three years the conservatives had been trying to maintain good relations with England and at the same time to combat what they considered the dangerous rising tide of radicalism in their own colonies. Now they were forced once more into opposition to England and so into unwilling alignment with the radicals.

The rest of the story is well-known by every schoolboy — how the tea was shipped over and refused admittance at every port; how Adams's followers in Boston raided the tea ship and threw fifty thousand dollars' worth of tea into the waters of the harbor; how Parliament, when it heard of the deed, passed acts closing the port to commerce except in food, until the tea should be paid for, voiding the Massachusetts charter, and placing the colony under the immediate control of the Crown, ordering that British officers or soldiers should be tried only in England (or in a colony other than Massachusetts) for anything done in the line of duty, and providing that troops should be quartered again in the colonies. "The die is cast," wrote George III to Lord North; "the colonies must either triumph or submit."

It is possible that a peaceful solution might have been found when the dull wits of the British Cabinet had become aware of the extent of feeling aroused in America, and of the fact that they had forced the whole population into a united front. But this would have been possible only had the tea not been destroyed, an act that many loyal Americans condemned. Adams had seized his chance. Fifty thousand dollars' worth of British private property destroyed and indemnity refused; Parliament would have to retaliate. If the retaliation should be heavy enough, the door might be closed to peaceful settlement. The retaliation came, swift and crushing, and the colonies were aflame with sympathy for Massachusetts. In the next three years the progress of events was inevitable in

its sequence, given all the factors involved. The petitions and their rejections, the calling of Congress, the bloodshed at Lexington and Concord, the final Declaration of Independence in 1776, and the military events of the struggle are too familiar to need retelling.

What concern us more particularly are the abiding influences upon American character and thought.

We have already seen how the wilderness and the colonists' need of erecting governments for themselves had given a considerable spur to the spread of democracy and the belief in government only by the consent of the governed. The colonies, however, had been far from democratic, and with the accumulation of wealth had been growing less so. Belief was still general among the upper classes that political power should rest in the hands of the well-born or the rich, who had knowledge, experience, and a property stake in the community. Many of the poorer classes, especially as we look further to the south from New England and out on any part of the frontiers, were shiftless, illiterate, rather lawless. To increase the political power of such people seemed to the conservatives like inviting anarchy and the spoliation of property. On the other hand, during the gradual shift in the grounds for arguing the constitutional relations toward Parliament, it had been found necessary to base the argument at last squarely on the rights of man. "When, in the course of human events," in the words of the great Virginian, it became necessary to inform the world why they were taking up arms against England, the signers of the Declaration had to announce the theory of these rights to all mankind — mankind including their own "lower classes" at home in America. "We hold these truths to be self-evident," wrote

Jefferson in words which rang through the continent, "that all men are created equal; that they are endowed by their Creator with certain inalienable rights; that among these are life, liberty, and the pursuit of happiness. That, to secure these rights, governments are instituted among men, deriving their just powers from the consent of the governed; that, whenever any form of government becomes destructive of these ends, it is the right of the people to alter or to abolish it."

Nothing here about the rich or the well-born; and, as Sam Adams said, the people recognized "the resolution as though it were a decree promulgated from heaven." The upper classes were thinking of their independence as against the exercise of legislative power by Parliament. The lower classes were thinking not only of that, but of their relations to their colonial legislature and governing class. "No taxation without representation." If that were true as between England and America, why not also as between poor Western frontier counties and rich Eastern seaboard ones, as between the town mechanic and the town merchant, as between the laborer and the planter?

If, as the King had said, the die was cast in imperial relations, so had it also been in American political philosophy. For a dozen years, men like Adams had been dinning this idea of the rights of man as man into the ears of the people. The conservatives had first been of the party, then fallen off, then again had to join it, and now at last the voice of united America in Congress had announced to the world the political equality of all men as the creed of the continent. The dam had been dynamited. After the announcement that all men are created equal, that all men have rights, that all men may revolt against conditions, there could be no turning back. The quarter of a century from the beginning of active agitation against England until the adoption of the Federal Constitution afforded an incomparable schooling in political discussion and training for an entire people, and for the burning into their minds and hearts of the democratic dogma.

Peter H. Odegard:

REVOLUTIONARY IDEAS, IDEALS, AND PROPAGANDA

THE long season of cynicism in our attitude toward propaganda, is happily coming to an end. The essentially sophomoric assumption that all propaganda is necessarily wicked is giving way to a more sensible appraisal of the function of propaganda in society. This new attitude enables us to pick and choose among competing propagandas and also consciously to use this ancient instrument for righteous ends instead of leaving it to be monopolized by the forces of darkness. I know of no better evidence of this mounting intellectual maturity than this excellent book on "Propaganda and the American Revolution."*

Propaganda has for centuries been prominent among the devices of diplomacy and it has been of ever increasing importance and effectiveness in war and revolution.

This is made brilliantly evident in Professor Davidson's book. It is especially reassuring now, when there is so much talk of the subtlety and efficiency of Nazi psychological warfare, to learn that our own revolutionary fathers were masters of the science and act of propaganda. At the outset of the revolution a small minority gradually they finally transformed an apathetic and somewhat reluctant majority into a united people and launched a great nation upon its dynamic and imperial course.

Their problems were not dissimilar from those which confront nearly every political propagandist — nor were the methods they employed markedly different. They had to justify their own objectives, demonstrate the value of these objectives to the people as a whole, arouse and sustain the will to resist by promoting hatred of the enemy, overcome or neutralize the propaganda of the opposition, and inculcate not only the illusion of victory but a sense of the inevitable triumph of their cause. To accomplish this they had, as must every successful revolutionary propagandist, a fertile soil in which to work. I think it was Harold Laski who said not long ago that even the skilled propagandist "does not influence the multitude unless the grievances for which he demands redress are grievances they profoundly feel."

The symbols and slogans which they used carried conviction because they were fortified by facts and events within the experience of nearly every colonist. There was widespread discontent with the Trade and Navigation Acts, the Grenville and Townsend Acts, the Stamp Act, and the innumerable stupidities of a mercantilist policy applied to a colonial economy lush in its readiness for laissez faire. There was the Boston Port Bill, the Quartering Act, and the incredible folly of the Boston Massacre. All of these

Reprinted by permission from the *Saturday Review of Literature*, XXV, No. 10 (March 7, 1942).
* [This is a review of *Propaganda and the American Revolution* by Philip Davidson (University of North Carolina Press, 1941).]

were grist for the propagandists' mill and they took full advantage of them.

But there was more than economic frustration to give substance to their symbols. There was the tradition of freedom reaching back to Magna Charta, the inalienable rights of Englishmen under the English Constitution, and the rapidly rising sun of eighteenth century liberalism and enlightenment. The propagandists took their ideological weapons from the arsenal of the enemy himself, from the writings of Coke and Blackstone, Bentham and John Locke. The American Revolution is but another illustration of the fact that there is nothing more irresistible than an idea whose time has come.

Every literate American has by now become familiar with the genius of Sam Adams as a walking delegate of revolution. One of the contributions made by Professor Davidson is that, without diminishing the credit due to Adams, he pays tribute to many able propagandists who aided him. Josiah Quincy the younger "could popularize a constitutional argument as well as anyone in the colonies and knew the central fact of crowd psychology — that emotion not reason, determines action." His appeal had all the more force because, together with John Adams, he had defended the soldiers accused of the Boston Massacre. Joseph Warren was another of the militant minority who stirred the laggard spirits of the colonists. "He used every position he held for the dissemination of propaganda, and not a committee he served on but became an agency for spreading the ideas of the radical party." It was he who cautioned the infants visiting the scene of their fathers' martyrdom after the Boston massacre to "take heed, lest . . . your feet slide on the stones bespattered with your fathers' brains."

Another was James Otis, "whose wild harangues in Boston town meeting did more for the cause among the lower people than did his bitter pamphlets. . . . His speeches against British officials were so inflammatory that mob action was almost inevitable." Joseph Hawley, Stephen Hopkins, William Livingston, William Gordon, Francis Hopkinson, John Trumbull, James Wilson, and Thomas Mifflin are among those less well known as propagandists. Not all their coadjutors were of their intellectual stamp and vigor. Samuel Chase of Maryland did not hesitate to lead a mob to demonstrate against the Stamp Act, Isaac Sears and Alexander McDougall of New York were mob masters with more courage and more integrity than most of their breed. Finally there was Tom Paine perhaps the greatest pamphleteer of his own or any time and certainly a true and perfect knight of freedom.

The machinery and techniques employed to communicate revolutionary symbols among the people are set forth by Davidson in great detail. They included the familiar committees of correspondence, churches, clubs, schools, and colleges, masonic lodges, workingmen's societies, and merchant organizations in nearly every colony and town. Other channels of communication and agitation included the Sons of Liberty, "the finest organization for the dissemination of propaganda among the working classes," the Mechanics Party, the Mohawk River Indians, the Philadelphia Patriotic Society, and many others.

Practically all the forty-two newspapers published in America in 1775 were under Whig control. "Not a single paper prior to 1774 was exclusively an organ of pro-British propaganda, and even after 1774 there were only a few." Their circulation was small by modern standards but their striking power was great and they probably had a greater secondary circulation than most newspapers today. Even more important, however, were the broadsides, pamphlets, and leaflets that were distributed by the thousands. Of these Tom Paine's "Common Sense" and Dickinson's "Letters from a Pennsylvania Farmer" are outstanding. Reprints of speeches and sermons were common.

The revolutionary propagandists labored under difficulties unknown to their contemporary prototypes. Transportation was primitive and slow at best. There were no radios, no moving pictures, no billboards, and the task of moulding and mobilizing the public opinion of widely scattered colonies and communities was a man-sized undertaking. But if the revolutionary fathers lacked skywriting and Donald Duck movies — they had the always effective parades, celebrations, mass meetings, demonstrations, songs, poems, plays, public addresses, and pulpit oratory and they used them all. Liberty Trees or Poles, cartoons, posters, and transparencies helped to give graphic representation to ideas. John Dickinson's "American Liberty Song" became immensely popular with its jingling rhyme of

Come join hand in hand, brave
    Americans all,
And rouse your bold hearts at fair
    Liberty's call. . . .

Nor was propaganda of the deed overlooked as the Boston Tea Party, innumerable hangings in effigy, and other activities for the release of muscular energy testify.

Most of the media open to the revolutionary leaders were closed to the Tories. "The Tory appeal," says Davidson, "was a written appeal; the dearth of oral dramatic, and pictorial suggestions is striking." Most effective of all for the loyalists were the sermons by Tory ministers, mainly Anglican and Presbyterian. Nevertheless the author does well to devote nearly a hundred pages to "Tory Counter Attack."

One of the striking things about the propaganda of the American Revolution is the timeless quality of much that has come down to us. "A spark of fire inflames a compact building, a spark of spirit will as soon enkindle a united people," wrote Josiah Quincy in 1773. It is as true today as then. Five years before, in 1768, he had written "By the sweat of our brow, we earn the little we possess; from nature, we derive the rights of man. . . . Shall we, dare we, pusillanimously, surrender our birthrights? . . . Answer me, thou coward! who hidest thyself in the hour of trial!"

There is a good deal more in this book that will repay reading in these troublous times. I commend it especially to those pseudo-realists who still believe that propaganda of all kinds is but a devil's brew from which no good can come. I commend it also to those who have forgotten that "in the beginning was the Word," and that words in the mouths of men of good will, faith, and courage can, even now, move mountains.

Suggestions for Additional Reading

A more elaborate presentation of Louis M. Hacker's economic interpretation will be found in Part II of his *The Triumph of American Capitalism* (New York, 1940). A very similar view is expressed by Charles A. and Mary R. Beard in Chapters 5 and 6 of *The Rise of American Civilization* (New York, 1934), which will also serve as an excellent narrative view of the period. For a full development of the views of John C. Miller and Claude H. Van Tyne, the reader should consult Miller's *Origins of the American Revolution* (Boston, 1943), and Van Tyne's *The Causes of the War of Independence* (Boston, 1922), from which the selections reprinted here have been taken. Charles M. Andrews has summarized his view in "The American Revolution: An Interpretation," *American Historical Review*, Vol. 31 (January, 1926); more extensive treatment is given in his *The Colonial Background of the American Revolution* (New Haven, 1931), particularly in the final two essays. H. E. Egerton, *The Causes and Character of the American Revolution* (Oxford and New York, 1923), and W. Alison Phillips, "The Declaration of Independence," *Edinburgh Review*, Vol. 244 (July, 1926), 1–17, represent two significant interpretations by British scholars, while Arthur M. Schlesinger's "The American Revolution" in his *New Viewpoints in American History* (New York, 1922) presents a further view, in which considerable stress is laid on the role of the merchants.

In most cases, the works mentioned offer interpretive or analytical, rather than narrative, treatment.

For more general considerations of the period, the reader would do well to consult Carl Becker, *The Eve of the Revolution* (New York, 1921), in which Becker shows the unfolding constitutional crisis as it might have appeared to Benjamin Franklin watching from England; and Evarts Boutell Greene, *The Revolutionary Generation, 1763–1790* (Vol. IV of *The History of American Life*, New York, 1943), in which the emphasis is on economic and social factors. Sydney George Fisher, *The Struggle for American Independence* (2 vols., Philadelphia, 1908), and Edward Channing, *A History of the United States* (New York, 1912), Vol. III, are still among the best general summaries of the period. An excellent summary of the sectional and class divisions of colonial America is to be found in Chapter III of Samuel Eliot Morison and Henry Steele Commager, *The Growth of the American Nation* (New York, 1937).

There are a number of studies which focus attention upon the influence of particular sections or classes. Among the most useful of these are James Truslow Adams, *Revolutionary New England, 1691–1776* (Boston, 1923), which is written with a distinct economic emphasis; Isaac Samuel Harrell, *Loyalism in Virginia* (Durham, N. C., 1926); and Arthur M. Schlesinger, *The Colonial Merchants and the American Revolution, 1763–1776*

(New York, 1918), which lends considerable support to the economic interpretation. Philip G. Davidson, *Propaganda and the American Revolution* (Chapel Hill, N. C., 1941), a review of which appears as the closing selection of these readings, offers an analysis of the ideas, symbols, and slogans of both revolutionists and Tories, and of the techniques and machinery used to win or to discourage support of the revolutionary cause. A good account of the military aspect of the conflict is to be found in Allen French, *The First Year of the American Revolution* (New York, 1934).

For more detailed analysis of the political and constitutional ideas of the Revolution, the reader should consult Charles H. McIlwain, *The American Revolution: A Constitutional Interpretation* (New York, 1923), and Randolph Greenfield Adams, *Political Ideas of the American Revolution*. Carl Becker, *The Declaration of Independence* (New York, 1933), examines the significance and the sources of the ideas embodied in that document. A good account of the natural law background of American political thought of the time is to be found in Benjamin F. Wright, Jr., *American Interpretations of Natural Law* (Cambridge, Mass., 1931), while Charles F. Mullett offers an analysis of the thought underlying British colonial policy in "English Imperial Thinking, 1764–1783," *Political Science Quarterly*, Vol. 45 (December, 1930).

Excellent collections of contemporary materials may be found in Henry Steele Commager, *Documents of American History* (New York, 1934); Albert Bushnell Hart, *American History Told by Contemporaries* (2 vols., New York, 1898); Samuel Eliot Morison, *Sources and Documents Illustrating the American Revolution, 1764–1788* (New York, 1929); and Benjamin F. Wright, Jr., *A Source Book of American Political Theory* (New York, 1929). An illuminating Report of the Boston Committee of Correspondence, written November 20, 1772, by Samuel Adams, is printed in part, together with Benjamin Franklin's Preface to the English edition of the Report, as *Old South Leaflet, No. 173* (Boston, n.d.).

The reader who wishes to compare the American Revolution with other great revolutions will find much to reward him in Crane Brinton, *The Anatomy of Revolution* (New York, 1938).